Bear

Animal
Series editor: Jonathan Burt

Already published

Crow
Boria Sax

Tortoise
Peter Young

Cockroach
Marion Copeland

Ant
Charlotte Sleigh

Dog
Susan McHugh

Oyster
Rebecca Stott

Forthcoming

Rat
Jonathan Burt

Parrot
Paul Carter

Snake
Drake Stutesman

Whale
Joe Roman

Falcon
Helen Macdonald

Bee
Claire Preston

Hare
Simon Carnell

Moose
Kevin Jackson

Fly
Steven Connor

Tiger
Susie Green

Fox
Martin Wallen

Crocodile
Richard Freeman

Cat
Katharine M. Rogers

Spider
Katja and Sergiusz Michalski

Duck
Victoria de Rijke

Peacock
Christine Jackson

Salmon
Peter Coates

Wolf
Garry Marvin

Bear

Robert E. Bieder

REAKTION BOOKS

Published by
REAKTION BOOKS LTD
79 Farringdon Road
London EC1M 3JU, UK
www.reaktionbooks.co.uk

First published 2005
Copyright © Robert E. Bieder 2005

Printed and bound in Singapore by CS Graphics

British Library Cataloguing in Publication Data
Bieder, Robert E.
    Bear. – (Animal)
    1. Bears 2. Animals and civilization
    I. Title
    599.7'8

    ISBN 1 86189 204 7

Contents

1　Ursidae

On a bright, hot, June morning, in the company of Professor László Kordos, paleontologist and Head of the Geological Museum of Hungary, and Professor Zoltán Abádi-Nagy of the University of Debrecen, I climbed a well-worn path to the large limestone Istállósko cave. Zoltán, an old friend, had put me in touch with Professor Kordos. After I spent some days studying cave bear skulls at the museum, László suggested a trip to the Bükk Mountains in northeastern Hungary to visit the Istállósko cave, the source of some of the cave bear remains that I had been looking at. This beautiful limestone mountain range with cascading streams extends along the border between Hungary and Slovakia. With other ranges it marks the northern limits of the Carpathian basin.

On either side of our narrow path, beech and pine trees marched up the hillside in irregular order and provided welcome shade. As we rounded a rock outcrop, suddenly the cave loomed into sight. We passed into the cave through an awesome portal reminiscent of the grand entrance into the banquet hall of Grieg's Hall of the Mountain King. On either side, the walls arched like a Gothic cathedral toward the ceiling while the uneven sandy floor sloped away, losing itself in the dark, cool shadows in the rear. The site of several successful digs for cave bear remains, the cave is about 100 feet deep and only half its original length,

A human form gives a sense of the scale of the Istállósko cave, Hungary, formerly a place of hibernation for the now-extinct cave bear.

the front half having long ago collapsed down the mountain. Our search along the walls of the cave, where bone fragments or molars would most probably be found, proved unsuccessful.

The cave bear, now extinct, disappeared only about 15,000 years ago, but did the hills I looked out on from the mouth of the cave hold the bones of bears that lived long before cave bears? How many species of bears wandered over the earth between the first bear and the cave bear? How did bears evolve?

The history of bears is measured in geological terms of millions of years; time spans often punctuated by ice ages when glaciers miles high covered much of the northern hemisphere and inter-glacial periods when the great ice sheets retreated. But the story of bears begins even before the glacial age, in the early Miocene, one of the great divisions of the Tertiary period, about 22 million years ago, when the first bear ancestor emerged in what later would become Europe.

What did *Ursavus* see? Certainly not the Europe we know today. Europe for the most part was a sub-tropical land mass. Britain was firmly attached to the continent by a land bridge to France. The Iberian Peninsula extended further both east and west. The Mediterranean Sea nearly covered Italy and bit deep into the coasts of France, Greece and Turkey. Warm breezes from the Atlantic, narrower than it is today, blew moisture across Europe that created lush tropical forests. Scandinavia and Finland were attached to Europe and the Baltic Sea was far in the future. Between Britain and Scandinavia a cold sea extended southward covering what is now part of the north German coast and most of Denmark. The Alps were just pushing up, forming a land mass between the Mediterranean and a large freshwater lake to the north. To the east of this lake, from southern France to Austria, a vast brackish sea covered much of southern Europe and extended into Asia, while a vast swamp covered northeastern Germany and Poland.

Paleontologists today see an explosion of essentially modern life forms during this period. At the end of the Oligocene, the period before the Miocene, about 25 million years ago, many of the creatures that inhabited that earlier world slid into extinction. But some creatures, including some mammals, continued into the Miocene, contributing to the rich variety of terrestrial life that characterized that period. The many limestone caves in western and central Europe served as homes for an array of creatures, including bear-dogs, weasels, foxes, skunk-like animals, early ancestors of the mongoose and numerous other small mammals, birds and reptiles. Among these creatures was one about the size of a fox terrier; scientists have named it *Ursavus elemensis*, sometimes called the 'dawn bear'. Many scientists see this creature as the beginning of the bear line.

So what did dawn bear look like? Did it look like a miniature bear? Did it climb trees? Did it have long, shaggy hair? We do not know. The only remains are its teeth and jaws. But paleontologists are some of the world's greatest detectives, creating whole animals from a tooth, a bone, a skull or a jaw. They also make guesses. Because dawn bear lived in heavily forested areas and bears – at least when young – are good climbers, *Ursavus* may also have been a good climber. *Ursavus* also probably dined on insects, small vertebrates and plants, but these are only guesses. What is known is that over the eons, dawn bear grew larger and its teeth grew more bear-like.[1]

Of all the physical remains of bears, probably the most important are teeth. When very old remains are found, bones may have largely disintegrated but the teeth (of all body parts the hardest) and their order in the skull, are often the only clue to species identification. In bear remains the teeth, especially the molars, can tell us not only what subspecies it belonged to, but something about the age of the animal when death occurred, its mode of life, and its eating pattern.

In time, dawn bear changed, but so did its world. Larger neighbours, mastodons, pushed into Europe from Africa, and the one-toed or hoofed horse, that would soon replace the three-toed horse, ambled in from North America. At a site called Can Llobateres, near the Spanish city of Sabadell just northeast of Barcelona, bones of several mammals including, gibbons and apes, provided proof that about 13 million years ago the region was still subtropical in climate and flora.

The collection of bones at this site near Barcelona also contained an unusual tooth. Not a lot can be learned from a single tooth, but paleontologists believe that it belonged to a bear-like creature. From its size, it is evident that the creature was larger than the dawn bear or *Ursavus elemensis* from which it may have descended, or else from other contemporary *Ursavi*. This new bear-like creature was given the name *Protursus simpsoni*, but although more advanced than other *Ursavi*, it did not reach the developmental stage of a true *Ursus.*

About 10 million years ago the European world became dryer. Subtropical plants and forests gave way to deserts, steppes and grass-covered plains. Such a world was ideal for early ruminants like antelopes and primitive horses, but not for forest-dwelling creatures like *Ursavus*, which became extinct. Around this time, another side branch of *Ursavi*, an early bear-like creature called *Indarctos*, spread from Asia into North America. The trail of the Spanish *Protursus* is lost at this time and is not picked up again until we pass from the Miocene into the Pliocene, about 5 million years ago, when it might have given rise to *Tremarctos*, which roamed the Americas.

In the Pliocene, a new bear-like creature, *Ursus minimus*, the first, smallest and most primitive of the *Ursus* family, approaching the size of today's small Malaysian sun bear, is found in both France and Hungary.

Once again, however, the climate changed. Out of the north, about 1.5 million years ago, sheets of ice began to pile up a mile high and creep ominously southward. The Ice Age had begun. In response to the bitter cold, many animals grew larger to better conserve body heat. New creatures – bison and oxen – began to roam across the steppes. From Africa, elephants and mammoths made their way northward. *U. minimus* also grew in size and began to travel into Asia, perhaps even into North America. It is probable that *U. minimus* or a closely related species gave rise to the American black bear, *Ursus americanus*, and in the Himalayan region to the Asian black bear, *Ursus thibetanus*, which spread throughout much of southeast Asia. There is molecular evidence that *U. minimus* is also the ancestor of *Ursus malayanus*, the Malaysian sun bear, and of *Ursus ursinus*, the sloth bear.

Bear evolution was also proceeding apace in Europe. About 2.5 million years ago, in the Villafranchian period, the now larger *U. minimus* gave rise to the even larger Etruscan bear, *Ursus etruscus*. This new bear spread from western Europe to China. The Etruscan bear, in size probably similar to the American black bear, wandered throughout much of Europe and Asia until about 1.5 million years ago, or to the end of the Tiglian interglacial that followed the Villafranchian age, and then exited the stage, a much larger creature than when it made its entrance. Now, a descendant of *U. etruscus*, *Ursus arctos*, began its history, one that would see it wander into the Americas. The prolific Etruscan bear gave rise to yet another, *Ursus savini*, about 1 million years ago; it died out about 700,000 years ago.

With *U. savini*, it is possible to glimpse the origin of the large European cave bear. The heightened domed forehead so characteristic of the cave bear makes its appearance. The tooth pattern is also similar to that of the cave bear. In the Waalian interglacial period, about 1 million years ago, the earth again began to warm and the mountains of ice retreated. Europe again filled up with animals, one of which, a long-legged bear, *Ursus deningeri*, began to supplant *U. savini*. This last interloper on the European scene may have evolved as early as the Günz Ice Age, nearly 1 million years ago, but hung on until the Cromerian interglacial, about 700,000 years ago. *U. deningeri*, larger than the Etruscan bear, not only probably gave rise to the giant cave bear but also encountered another creature coming out of Africa – early human precursors; perhaps an early form of Neanderthal man.

As *U. deningeri* lumbered across Europe carrying many features of the cave bear, like the longer jaw, Europe began to feel the

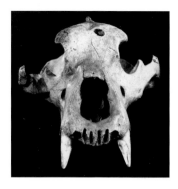

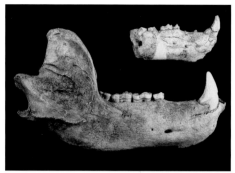

A cave bear skull from the front.

Lower jaws of the cave bear and its predecessor, the Etruscan bear.

chill of yet another long, cold 'winter'; the Elster glaciation. When it finally warmed up again in the Holsteinian interglacial, about 300,000 years ago, a new bear, much larger than *U. deningeri*, emerged. This was the great European cave bear, or *Ursus spelaeus*. The cave bear possessed a high-domed, massive skull with large grinding teeth and also a thick, heavy lower jaw. The sagittal crest, a bone ridge that runs the length of the dome part of the skull from front to back, is extremely prominent, as are the wide-splayed zygotic arches on either side of the skull that gave the bear an awesome appearance in life. The thick lower jaw and

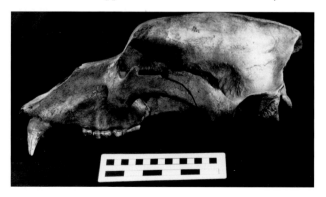

A cave bear skull from the side, showing the high domed massive skull with pro-nounced 'sagittal crest' running from front to back.

sagittal crest served as bases to anchor the powerful chewing muscles. The zygotic arches are splayed wide to allow the muscles to pass underneath. Such large chewing muscles and the bear's well-developed grinding molars indicate that much of its diet consisted of vegetation, especially in spring and summer. According to Professor Kordos, cave bears probably complemented their predominately vegetable diet with meat in the fall.[2]

The wandering of *U. spelaeus* stretched across Europe from Spain to Euroasia: from Italy and Greece to Belgium, the Netherlands and, perhaps, Britain, across much of Germany into Poland, and then south into Hungary, Romania and parts of Russia. No traces have been found in northern Britain, Scandinavia or the Baltic countries, which were then still covered with extensive glaciers. The cave bear could be found in low mountain areas and especially in regions of extensive limestone caves. It seemed to avoid the open plains and preferred forest or forest-edge habitation.

The greatest number of cave bear remains is found in Austria, Switzerland, southern Germany, northern Italy, northern Spain, Croatia, Hungary and Romania. In many of the caves throughout south, central and east Europe, the huge number of remains has led some to think that at one time Europe literally possessed herds of cave bears. However, although many caves contain thousands of cave bear bones, these bones were deposited over a period of 100,000 years or even longer, and all it would take was the death of one or two bears a year in a cave to account for the thousands of remains.

But if there were only a few bears in a particular region at any given time, they did not lack for the company of other animals. Their neighbours were many and sometimes very large: lions larger than any existing today, giant bison, straight-tusked elephants, woolly rhinoceros, giant deer, hippopotami, wolves and cave hyenas. But few animals of the time would have been foolish enough to attack a cave bear. Those animals, however, that hunted in groups – wolves and hyenas – would sometimes chance an encounter, especially if the bear was old, lame, diseased, very young, or if the sovereignty of the cave was in question.

The longevity of the cave bear is not known. It was estimated by the late Finnish paleontologist Björn Kurtén that they seldom exceeded 20 years of age,[3] calculating that by that time their molars would have been ground down to stumps, making it difficult to eat. Worn teeth posed only one problem. Tooth abcesses leading to blood poisoning was one cause of death, while osteoarthritis, osteolysis, fractures, rickets and many other bone diseases, especially in the forearms resulting from heavy use, also led to weakened physical condition and death. Death also occurred from falling rocks during hibernation.

Why the cave bear became extinct, probably about 10,000 years ago, is still a mystery. Some feel their large size and lack of enemies caused degeneration in the species, but many dispute this. Some claim the loss of habitat to support the population due to changing climate was the main cause, but others note that the cave bear had survived other times of climatic change. Extinction due to overhunting by early humans is ruled out since the human population was too small at that time to make such inroads into the bear population although, undoubtedly, there were disputes over cave ownership. As Kurtén notes, 'By and large, the Ice Age hunting people probably lived in harmony with their environment, harvesting the surplus rather than making inroads on the capital.'[4]

There are other tentative theories. According to Kurtén, many local cave bear populations were fragmented, under stress, or had disappeared even before the advent of the glaciers. Thus, according to Kurtén, the cave bear was an endangered

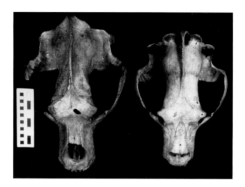

Skulls of the cave bear (*left*) and the brown bear.

species prior to the period of dramatic climate change. Many other large animals besides the cave bear also became extinct at the end of the Ice Age – mammoths, leopards, woolly rhinos and stepped bison, to name but a few. Probably a combination of factors killed off the cave bear. The end of the Ice Age, changing climate affecting habitats, and fragmented populations, all may have pushed the last remnant of the cave bear population beyond the pale.[5]

As the cave bear exited the stage, *Ursus arctos*, or the European brown bear, became the largest bear in Europe. *U. arctos*, as we have seen, came on the scene earlier than the cave bear, descending from *U. etruscus* around 1.5 million years ago. The European brown bear had a much larger range than the cave bear and eventually inhabited most of Europe, where it still resides in limited numbers in Scandinavia, Finland, Russia, Spain, Italy, France and Romania. It also exists in northern Asia and North America. In the latter continent it still roams as the grizzly and the large Kodiak bear of Alaska. *U. americanus*, or the American black bear, also made the long journey from Asia to North America, probably thousands of years before the brown bear migrated.

Shifting to the western hemisphere, we find bears unlike any that appeared in Europe or Asia. The Americas served as host to the subfamily of the Ursidae, the Tremarctinae. This subfamily included *Tremarctos floridanus*, or the giant Florida cave bear, which was similar in height and weight to the European cave bear. Five other members were the short-faced bears *Arctodus simus*, *A. pristinus*, *A. bonariensis*, *A. pamparus* and *A. brasiliensis*. The bones of the giant Florida cave bear evince a body built for strength and power – but not for speed – and adapted to the ecological niche in which it lived. Was there a relationship between the Florida cave bear and the European cave bear, which it closely resembled? If so, how did they come to inhabit such widely different ecologies? The answer to the first question is maybe, but the divergence between the two probably took place about 10 million years ago, or even earlier, when both descended from an earlier type. How *T. floridanus* came to take up residence in North America is not known, nor is it known when this species became extinct. Remains of this bear have been found with those of early humans in North America, so it could have moved through the southeastern parts of what is now the United States as recently as a few thousand years ago.

A still larger bear also roamed North America. This was *A. simus*, or the giant short-faced bear. As noted above, four other short-faced bears lived in the western hemisphere; *A. pristinus* in North America and *A. bonariensis*, *A. pamparus* and *A. brasiliensis* in South America. The most impressive, however, was *A. simus*. Weighing in at an estimated 2,200 lb (1,000 kg), this long-legged bear would dwarf all of today's bears. It was the largest and most powerful bear that ever lived. Given its long legs, many believe it must have been fleet-footed and most probably a carnivore. Evidence from the skull and jaw indicate that it had an exceptionally powerful

Ursidae Family

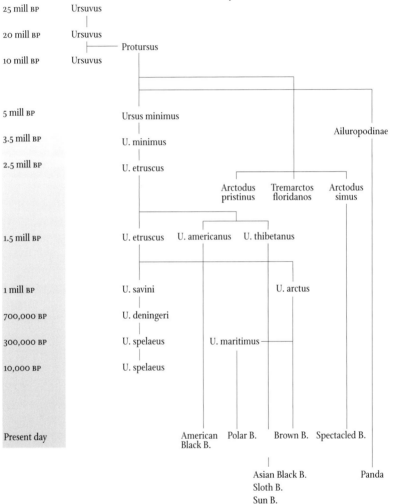

25 mill BP	Ursuvus	
20 mill BP	Ursuvus	
		Protursus
10 mill BP	Ursuvus	
5 mill BP	Ursus minimus	
3.5 mill BP	U. minimus	Ailuropodinae
2.5 mill BP	U. etruscus	
		Arctodus pristinus Tremarctos floridanos Arctodus simus
1.5 mill BP	U. etruscus U. americanus U. thibetanus	
1 mill BP	U. savini U. arctus	
700,000 BP	U. deningeri	
300,000 BP	U. spelaeus U. maritimus	
10,000 BP	U. spelaeus	
Present day	American Black B. Polar B. Brown B. Spectacled B.	
	Asian Black B. Sloth B. Sun B. Panda	

bite. Its remains are found in sites from California to Maryland and Pennsylvania, and from Mexico to Alaska. Again, when this bear became extinct is unknown. Considering the large size of all the bears in this subfamily, it is surprising that many think one of its distant descendants is the small spectacled bear, or *Tremarctos ornatus*, which today roams parts of South America.

Probably the first bears that European hominids encountered were the cave bear and the brown bear. Although not found as frequently as other animals in European cave paintings, bears are represented. Most of the paintings, however, seem to be of brown bears. According to Kurtén, there are few paintings of cave bears. Does this indicate that the smaller brown bears proved easier to hunt? Were brown bears more numerous than cave bears or did the ecosphere of humans and brown bears coincide more closely than that of humans and cave bears? These are questions for which no answers exist at present.

With this brief ramble across four continents and roughly 22 million years of bear history, there are, without doubt, not only omissions of facts but perhaps even of some bear species here and there. The future will add to our knowledge as paleontologists or archaeologists uncover further bear species. When they do, current interpretations will change. As one student of bears pointed out: 'The fossil record of bears is incomplete and leaves unanswered a considerable number of questions about the ancestral relationships between the eight species that are living today.'[6] What is known is that the family Ursidae contains the largest carnivorous land mammal to exist both in the fossil record and in the present day. This story that began for me on a June morning in Hungary at the Istállósko cave continues with a look at the survivors of the Ursidae family.

The upper dentition of the (extinct) cave bear, showing the large canines and molars.

The upper dentition of a male and a female brown bear

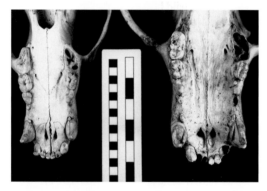

The upper dentition of the polar bear, showing small molars.

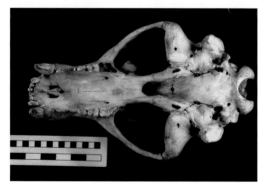

2 Survivors

An ancient Greek alchemist once said, describing a bear: 'The bear is a shaggy, slothful, wild beast, in all respect like a man, and wishful to walk upright.'[1] A shrewd observation, but is the bear really 'in all respect like a man'? What are the physical characteristics that set bears apart from humans or, for that matter, from other species?

We have already mentioned that tooth pattern is important for identification of species and subspecies. Bears have large canine teeth for grabbing and holding prey, which are also useful to intimidate other animals and to defend themselves. But bears, like humans, are omnivores – they also eat plants – so canine teeth are no good for eating the plants, roots, nuts, berries and insects that constitute most bears' principal diets. For these foods, their molars are more useful, since they are designed for grinding up vegetable matter. Plant cells are much more difficult for the digestive system to break down than animal cells. Humans cook vegetables to start the cellular breakdown process, but bears can only grind plant food with their large molars. Molars reduced to stumps or worn down even below the crown line are often found in the skulls of old bears. Large molars are found in all bears with the exception of the polar bear. This is because it is the only true carnivore; the only bear that depends primarily on animal food.[2]

Besides large canines, bears share another physical attribute with carnivores. Carnivores, as opposed to herbivores, have short intestines. Where herbivores like horses and cows have intestines 20 to 25 times their body length, bears' intestines are only 6 to 10 times their body length. Surprisingly, pandas, *Ailuropoda melandeuca*, the most herbivorous of the Ursidae family, have the shortest intestines, only four to five times their body length.[3]

There are many other similarities among bears. All have large heads, small ears, and short backs and tails. Despite their small ears, bears have an extraordinarily acute sense of hearing. They have an even better sense of smell, which allows them to detect game a mile away. Polar bears are said to be able to locate seals by their scent through two feet of ice and snow. All bears also have thick muscular legs and, except for polar bears, massive shoulders.[4] The claws of bears are not retractile.

Bears are not built for speed. However, as many bear watchers have learned, if they penetrate a bear's sense of private space, they are unlikely to escape its charge. Bears can easily outrun humans. They can also run down old, weak or very young hoofed animals, but prefer to hunt by stratagem and ambush. Many bears, although not all, can climb trees. Some can climb only when they are young and lose the ability as they age. People have escaped death from a charging bear by climbing high into a tree in the nick of time. Others, not realizing how far a large bear can reach up when standing on its hind legs, have suffered injuries. In most cases, when given sufficient warning, or if their cubs are not threatened, bears prefer to move off.

All modern bears belong to a group known as plantigrade mammals. Like humans, bears walk on the soles of their feet and not on their toes, as do digitigrade animals such as horses, dogs and cats. It is this plantigrade trait that allows bears to stand up and walk on their hind legs. Another trait that distinguishes

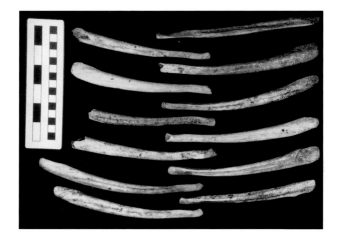

Male bears have long, elliptical curved penis bones ('baculi').

male bears are long, round, slender bones in their penises called baculi. These are characteristic of species where ovulation is induced through intercourse. The baculum is thought to provide the longer and more intense stimulation needed for ovulation. Female bears undergo delayed implantation of fertilized eggs, whereby a fertilized egg floats for a period of time before attaching itself to the uterus wall. Because mating takes place in the late spring or early summer and cubs are not born until the following winter or early spring, delayed implantation allows the females time to store the fat that will sustain them through pregnancy and acquire the strength needed to give birth – for they do not eat at all during this period. Female bears are in oestrus for only a short period of time but ovulation does not occur until it is induced by mating. Hence mating continues over several days in order to stimulate the ovaries into egg production.

Ursidae intelligence is often underrated in literature. Although in many animal fables bears are depicted as not very bright and suffering from the pranks of other species, this does not reflect the

Mating brown bears.

intelligence of real bears. Early western literature, taking its cue from even earlier fables, characterized bears as slow, both mentally and physically. This is staunchly denied by hunters and those who train bears for circuses and movies. Hunters report that bears they track in snow can backtrack in their own footprints, thus throwing pursuers off their trails. Native Americans claim that old bears do not go into their dens head first once snow has fallen but instead back into the den, leaving tracks that appear to be heading out of it. Inuit people claim that they learned to hunt seals by watching how bears do it.

Contrary to reports that bears have poor eyesight, their vision is probably comparable to that of humans. They excel at detecting even the slightest of movements. Accounts of poor eyesight perhaps arose because bears seldom look directly at humans or even at other bears. To do so, in Ursidae terms, is to issue a direct challenge. There are still arguments over whether all bears have colour vision. It is known that black bears do, and most scholars agree that other bears can distinguish at least some colours.

Many people associate bears with hibernation, yet not all bears hibernate. Hibernation is thought to result from a lack of food. Except for polar bears, *Ursus maritimus*, bears that live in temperate climates go into hibernation when winter snow covers or destroys the vegetation upon which they so heavily depend. Polar bears, except for pregnant females, do not den up over the winter since that is the time when hunting is most productive. In late spring, summer and early autumn when bears in temperate climates find abundant food, polar bears find hunting difficult. They live mostly on seals, which they hunt on Arctic ice packs. When summer warmth breaks up these packs and turns the ice fields into open sea, hunting becomes difficult, if not impossible.

But polar bears are not the only ones that do not hibernate. Ursidae members living in the rainforests of South America, Southeast Asia or in the hot regions of the Indian subcontinent,

The polar bear, one of the eight currently extant sub-species of bear.

also do not hibernate, or only for short periods of time to give birth. In areas with a plentiful food supply all year round, there is no need to hibernate, and in order to do so for long periods of time, bears need to store up vast amounts of body fat. During hibernation, bears lose between 30 and 50 per cent of their weight. But bears that feed primarily upon plants, fruits and insects are unable to build up layers of fat in the same way as those who feed on salmon, nuts, plants and other animals.

Many cultures have perceived a similarity between bears and humans. This topic will be considered later, but disease is one area that bears definitely share with humans since they, too, suffer from arthritis, tuberculosis, bronchopneumonia, dental cavities and haemorrhoids. Besides being plagued also with ticks, fleas and lice, bears are host to intestinal flukes and worms, including the roundworm, *Trichinella*, which causes trichinosis. It is estimated that all polar bears and threequarters of all brown bears suffer from this disease.

As with most families, so with the Ursidae: while there are similarities among its members, there are also differences. Some are small in stature, others large. Some prefer to dine on leaves, berries, nuts and insects, while others feed almost entirely on meat. The smallest member of the Ursidae family, the sun bear, *U. malayanus* of Southeast Asia, is about the size of a very large dog, weighing between 60 and 120 lb (27–65 kg). Its northern cousin, the polar bear, is awesomely huge. Standing on its hind legs, *U. maritimus* can measure 8 ft or more (2.4–2.6 m), and males weigh from 800 to 1,320 lb (400–600 kg). Polar bears are the largest carnivores on earth. The sun bear and the polar bear, however, constitute only two of the eight living species of Ursidae.

The sun bear is now increasingly difficult to find in the wild, and is the least known of the Ursidae family. Its home is the rainforests of southeast Asia, including Malaysia, Myanmar (Burma), Bangladesh, Laos, Cambodia, Thailand, Vietnam and Indonesia. Its name derives from a yellow crescent emblazoned across its chest. In Thailand, it is known as the dog bear in reference to its small size and the short hair that is characteristic of a hound or terrier. Many Malaysians call it the honey bear or Malay bear. The sun bear's hairless footpads, long, curved claws, and short, bowed legs make it perfectly adapted to climbing. On the ground, this bear sets a frenetic pace at night in its search for insects, small rodents, lizards, small birds, eggs, earthworms, fruit, termites and honey.[5]

Although small, the sun bear, once aroused, can be a formidable adversary: 'The sun bear is said to be one of the most dangerous animals a human can encounter in the jungle.'[6] It possesses exceptionally strong jaws and long claws that can tear logs apart and deliver deep, slashing cuts. It is said that even tigers prefer to avoid mounting an attack. Despite the sun bear's small physical size, its canine teeth compare favourably with those of lions and tigers. Scientists do not know why it has such large canines since its diet consists primarily of insects and fruits. Some claim that the sun bear is exceptionally aggressive and will attack without cause. If so, its long canine teeth would come in handy. It may also display them when assuming a threatening stance.[7]

When not scurrying around the rainforest floor, sun bears are nesting in trees. Generally nocturnal in their feeding habits, during the day they can often be found on crude platforms or nests sometimes as high as 20 ft (6 m) above the ground. Here they rest, sleep or sunbathe.

Little is known about sun bear reproductive habits. In zoos, their gestation periods have ranged from 95 to 240 days (the latter figure suggests delayed implantation). It seems repro-

The sun bear. Note the large claws.

duction is not linked to a seasonal cycle as it is with many other bears, but determined by the availability of fruits or insects. Nor do sun bears give birth in dens. Instead, they give birth to two or three cubs in secluded arbours. Each cub weighs about 10 oz (325 g) at the time of birth, and they are thought to stay with the mother until fully grown.[8]

Next in size is the giant panda, *Ailuropoda melanodeuca*, which today inhabits the remote, inhospitable mountain ranges of

The giant panda.

A Han dynasty Chinese sculpture of a female bear.

western China. For many years, the panda was not thought to be a bear but a member of the raccoon family. Scientists now conclude that it is indeed a bear. Many people worldwide are familiar with its striking black and white markings; it is a popular stuffed animal toy and the logo of the WWF (formerly the World Wildlife Fund). The panda is probably the most popular bear of the Ursidae family and is a favourite at those zoos fortunate enough to obtain pandas from China (generally on loan for a certain number of years).

A Qing dynasty Chinese court official's insignia of rank, showing a bear.

The panda's debut on the stage of history is, like the mountains they inhabit, shrouded in mist. Early records are vague and inconclusive. The earliest mention of pandas is from about 4,000 years ago, when panda skins were sent as a tribute to a Chinese emperor. However, this account may lie more in the realm of legend than in fact. Later accounts from around 623 AD carry more weight, but here, too, there is confusion.

Records speak of a white bear skin from the mountains of China's Szechuan province near its border with Tibet. But could the provenance be mistaken and the white bear be a polar bear, also known in China at that time? The Italian explorer Marco Polo wrote of seeing polar bears in China, but did he really see pandas? The Silk Road, the main artery for trade between China and the Middle East, ran partly through panda country. Since skins and furs were bundled up with other products that made up the trade from China to the West, might panda skins and perhaps live animals have constituted part of the trade? The first reliable account of pandas reaching the West is that of Père Armand David, a French missionary, naturalist and explorer who obtained a panda skin in China in 1869 and sent it to the Paris Museum of Natural History.[9]

Pandas split off from the main Ursidae line in the Miocene, about 10 million years ago. Although they may eat some carrion, their diet consists almost entirely of about 30 different species of bamboo. They are the most vegetarian bear of their family. Such a diet is reflected in the panda's physiology. Their heads are large compared to the rest of the body, housing sizeable muscles on either side of the skull for chewing. Their molars offer a large surface for chopping, grinding and crushing bamboo branches, stems and leaves. Because pandas retain the intestines of the carnivore order, they spend more time eating than other bears. Whereas herbivores have special intestines to help them digest cellulose, pandas lack these. And pandas can only digest about 21 per cent of what they eat, so they must ingest vast quantities of food and eat it quickly. It is estimated that an adult panda weighing about 220 lb (100 kg), must eat 26 to 33 lb (12 to 15 kg) of bamboo leaves and stems each day – even more if the diet consists of bamboo shoots only. Because the energy derived from their ingestion of bamboo nearly equals the amount of energy pandas require to sustain life, their nutritional margin of safety is very small.

Aiding the panda in acquiring its daily food quota is what appears to be a thumb on each of its front paws. Whereas primates have four fingers and an opposable thumb on each hand, pandas have five digits on each front paw and a thumb-like appendage which is really an outgrowth of a wrist bone called the radial sesamoid. This bone, enlarged and elongated, allows pandas to grasp and negotiate bamboo stalks when eating.[10]

Pandas are solitary animals except at mating time. The range of a male panda often overlaps with the smaller ranges of three or four females. Despite this proximity, they seldom meet. They communicate sexual readiness by rubbing a substance secreted from glands located in the anal-genital area on tree trunks or rocks. Sexual responsiveness in female pandas generally occurs in the spring.

Females seek out caves or hollow trees for giving birth to tiny cubs (often twins), that weigh only about 3 or 4 oz (85 to 140 g) each. Generally, a female panda will only raise one cub, leaving the other to die. A cub is weaned at about a year and a half. Both sexes mature in a time range from about four and a half to six and a half years. Sexual activity for males begins about their fifth year and continues until about fifteen. Peak reproductive years for females are between eight and eleven. In the wild, pandas rarely live longer than 22 years. Like the sun bear, they do not appear to hibernate. Given their diet and energy needs, pandas never build up enough fat to enable them to stop eating entirely for several weeks.[11]

The next largest bear is the Asiatic black bear. Males weigh from 220 to 440 lb (100 to 200 kg), while females, as usual, are

smaller. The bear is black, with a large white 'V' mark on its chest, a brown muzzle, and brown ears. Because of this white 'V' or crescent on the chest, it is known in some places as the moon bear. Its range in Asia is divided. One half extends from the low mountains of Afghanistan and Pakistan through northern India, Nepal and down into Myanmar (Burma), Thailand, Cambodia and Vietnam. The other spreads from northeast China into southern Russia, Taiwan and parts of Japan. Asian black bears prefer to live in the deciduous forests off low mountain areas.[12]

Asiatic black bears are primarily herbivores and feed on a range of plants, including fruits, nuts and bamboo. Males will roam over an area of 14 square miles (37 km²), to locate food at the times plants reach their peak in nutritional value. Besides plants, the Asiatic black bear may also feed upon bees' nests, insects, small animals and carrion. Because those living in the northern range must put on as much fat as possible before going into hibernation, they use their climbing ability to seek out walnuts, cedar, beech and pine nuts, all rich in fats and carbohydrates.[13]

With their exceptionally strong front legs, Asiatic black bears excavate winter dens for hibernation. Hollow trees also suffice. Females give birth in January. At birth, the cubs weigh about 10 oz (300 g), and like other bear cubs are blind and helpless. By the time they emerge from the den in March or April they weigh 4 to 6 lb (2 to 3 kg). Asiatic black bears living in the tropical rainforests of southeast Asia do not usually hibernate.

The sloth bear, *U. ursinus*, is the fourth largest of the Asian bears, with males between 175 to 310 lb (80–140 kg), females less. Its range is primarily the Indian subcontinent, Nepal and the island of Sri Lanka. Sloth bears have a rather comical appearance, because their shaggy, longhaired coats – which range in colour from black to reddish brown – appear under perpetual attack from a violent wind storm. Like Asiatic black bears, sloth bears have a white crescent on their chests. Their muzzles are long and flexible, resembling a garden hose, and end in noses that they can not only close voluntarily, preventing attacks from ants and termites, their favourite food, but can also twist from side to side.

The sloth bear.

Sloth bears consume incredible amounts of insects. Their forefeet are exceptionally strong, with three-inch claws enabling them to rip apart a termite nest. Their mouths are adapted for dining on insects. The sloth bear's lips are naked and can be made to protrude and its mouth contains no upper incisor teeth. These characteristics allow the bear to turn its mouth into a tube, which it uses to blow away dirt and vacuum up termites.[14]

The name sloth bear is the result of mistaken identity. When reports of this bear, along with skins, first reached Europe at the end of the eighteenth century, its strange physical appearance – especially its long curved claws – prompted Europeans to identify it as a giant sloth and give it the name *Ursine beadypus* (*beadypus* is the scientific name of the American sloth). Upon further study, they discovered the animal's more bear-like characteristics and changed its scientific name to *Melursus ursinus*, later to *U. ursinus*. But the common name stuck.[15]

Sloth bears fill a particular environmental niche. In a place where tigers, leopards and wild dogs hunt hoofed animals, where wild pigs eat tubers and roots, and where carrion rots quickly under the hot tropical sun, the bear's diet of ants, termites and fruit enables it to exploit food sources other animals reject. To feed on such delicacies, sloth bears require a sizeable domain. A minimum area for males was discovered to be about 3.7 square miles (10 km²), with females requiring a smaller area. Depending on the season, the male and female domains can overlap.

Sloth bears give birth to two cubs in the late fall or winter after a gestation period of six to seven months. Young cubs often ride on their mother's back, either to be transported from one feeding area to another, or for protection. They generally stay with their mother for two and a half years and after they are left on their own may remain together for another year.[16]

The American black bear, *U. americanus*, the next largest, comes closest to being a 'designer' bear. It comes in several colours – black, cinnamon, honey, blue and white. Its range extends from the Pacific to the Atlantic Ocean and from the Arctic tree-line in Canada and Alaska to the Gulf of Mexico. A few can even be found in the forested parts of the American southwest and in the tundra regions of northeast Canada. The colour variation in the black bear is associated with its habitat. The black variety is found in the eastern United States and eastern Canada. Brown, cinnamon and honey-coloured black bears are found in the western part of North America and especially in areas where they compete with grizzly bears. The blue-coloured black bear, known in some places as the glacier bear, gets its name from long white or yellow guard hairs that cover a deep blue-black undercoat. It is found only in the glaciated areas of Alaska, British Columbia and the Canadian Yukon. The white black bear, also called the Kermode bear or spirit bear by some American Indians, is found along the north-central coast of British Columbia. Colours can vary from a pure white to light red, pale yellow or light orange. Female Kermode bears can give birth to cubs with the same colorations or to brown and black ones.[17]

Black bears are extremely intelligent – some consider them the most intelligent of all bears. They are exceedingly agile and dexterous and, with their long claws, excellent climbers. They prefer dark, deciduous forests or swampy habitats and are generally nocturnal in their foraging and eating habits. Exactly when they arrived in North America from Asia is unknown. Black bears hibernate during the winter months, often using hollow trees and brush piles, but preferring holes in living trees, caves or dens dug in the earth. Female black bears may give birth about every two years depending on the nutritional status

The American black bear.

of their environment. Females are more selective in seeking out an area to build a den than males and put a priority on concealment and safety.

An adult male black bear weighs between 130 and 310 lb (59 to 140 kg); females less. Food consists of berries, nuts, fruit and grass, and insects such as ants and wasps. Like most bears, they love honey. They also eat garbage if they live near human settlements. In the spring or early summer, deer fawns, moose calves and beavers are added to their menus. Black bears reach maturity in about four years and females reach reproductive age in their third or fourth year, although, where food is abundant, some may reach sexual maturity after about two years.[18]

If the American black bear is the 'designer' bear, the South American spectacled bear is the 'ornamental' bear. As if to underscore this point, its scientific name is *Tremarctos ornatus* or ornamental bear. The spectacled bear, sometimes called the

Andean bear, is now the only bear found in South America. It ranges from Panama and Venezuela through the countries along the west coast of South America, and is even found in Argentina. Both its scientific and common names are derived from its distinct facial markings. The bear can be black or dark brown, but sports white or cream markings on its chest and face and swirls of white encircling its eyes, which give it the appearance of wearing spectacles or glasses. The spectacled bear is the third largest bear, with adult males weighing between 220 and 340 lb (100 to 154 kg), and standing 32 inches (just under a metre) high at the shoulders. Besides its idiosyncratic markings, the spectacled bear is distinctive in another way: many claim it is the last descendant either of the short-faced giant bear *A. simus*, or the South American variety, *A. pristinus*. The former, as noted in the last chapter, was the largest bear that ever walked the earth. The much smaller spectacled bears have long claws and are the most arboreal of all bears. They are most often found high in the trees of the rainforests.

Although the spectacled bear can be found in various habitats from mountain forests to deserts, its preferred environments are

The spectacled bear, from Geoffroy Saint-Hilaire and Frédéric Cuvier's 1824 *Histoire naturelle des mammifères*.

The brown bear.

the cloud rainforests of western South America, from 6,000 to 8,800 ft (approx. 1,800 to 2,700 m) above sea level. The bear's diet is varied and extensive, including deer, rabbits, vicuña, calves, birds, berries, cacti, fruits, plants, grasses and bulbs. To gather this diet, spectacled bears range widely and do most of their foraging at night. During the day they sleep in the large nests they construct in trees.[19]

Mating season is from mid to late spring. Unfortunately, the shrinking number of spectacled bears in the wild leaves many questions regarding their reproduction unanswered. It is believed that spectacled bears, like others, are characterized by delayed egg implantation. A litter of two or three cubs is born during the rainy season from November to February.[20]

Next in size is the brown bear. The Tlingit of Alaska say, 'People must always speak carefully of bear people since bears [even far away] have the power to hear [understand] human speech. Even though a person murmurs only a few careless words, the bear will take revenge.'[21] The Alaskan brown bear and its close relative the grizzly are considered by most North American Indians as very powerful 'people', on a level with shamans in their ability to control the supply of animals, to heal, to prophesy the future and govern the seasons. Some Asian people today hold similar ideas about the brown bear.

On 5 May 1805, Meriwether Lewis of the Lewis and Clark Expedition – the first to cross the American continent – wrote:

A clay pot ornamented with a bear paw, by an American southwest Pueblo Indian.

Cap[tain] Clark and Drewyer killed the largest brown bear this evening, which we have yet seen. [I]t was a most tremendious looking anamal and extreemly hard to kill notwithstanding he had five balls through his lungs and

Ari-Wa-Kis (Young Bull), an Oto-Pawnee Indian, photographed in 1913 wearing his bear-claw necklace.

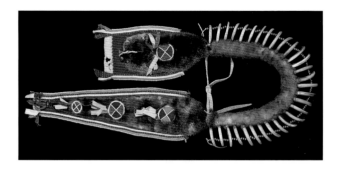

five others in various parts he swam more than half the
distance across the river [Missouri] to a sandbar, and it
was at least twenty minutes before he died . . .

The Native Americans had warned Lewis and Clark about these
gigantic grizzlies but they had not believed them.[22] For many
Native Americans of the Great Plains, the grizzly bear was the
most ferocious of all game, and the wearing of a grizzly claw
necklace evinced extreme bravery and skill.

The respect bestowed on the brown bear is an enduring
measure of its strength and spiritual power. *U. arctos* is a formidable animal – large, strong and quick – and the second largest
carnivore on earth. Its range once extended across Europe from
England to northern Asia and into North America, but is now
only a fraction of this. Only about 500 brown bears are left in
central and western Europe. A few are found in Spain, Italy and
the Alps, mostly in the mountain regions, while larger populations exist in Scandinavia, Russia, and the Carpathian and
Balkan mountains. Still others can be found on the Japanese
island of Hokkaido. The largest numbers today are in Siberia
and North America, especially in the mountains of the American
and Canadian West and in Alaska. A debate exists among tax-

onomists over the classification of the brown bear. Some recognize two subspecies. One, *Ursus arctos horribilus*, includes the grizzly bear and the large Kodiak bears of Alaska. The second places the Japanese bears under the separate nomenclature, *Ursus arctos middendorffi*. Others want to label the European brown bear *Ursus arctos arctos*, and the Japanese bear *Ursus arctos yesoensis*.

Despite the discrepancy in scientific identifications, there are no major differences among the groups that constitute *U. arctos* except weight. The large size of the Kodiak bear is a matter of diet. Living in an area where millions of spawning salmon constitute the bulk of the bears' food for part of a season, this bear grows extremely large, much larger than the grizzly which is forced to depend on berries, roots, nuts, insects, grubs and, to a lesser extent, on killing or scavenging on the winter kill remains of deer, elk or moose. The largest brown bears are reported from coastal Alaska where males can weigh 860 lb (390 kg), and females 455 lb (206 kg). Large males, as one would expect, are better able to acquire a mate or mates, while large females produce a greater number of young and are better able to protect them. Compared to the European brown bear, American bears are more aggressive. Whether this is because European bears have been hunted by humans over a longer period of time or because the larger size of the American brown bear makes for more aggressive behaviour is unknown.

Because bears are driven constantly to finding food, they tend to be loners, wandering over large areas in their gustatory pursuit. Their large teeth, formidable claws, strength, acute senses of hearing and smell and, for some, their ability to explode in short bursts of speed reaching 50 miles per hour (80 km/h) for short distances, make them exceptional killing machines. Yet, bears derive as much as 60 to 90 per cent of their diets from vegetative sources. Since the bulk of bears' diet consists of such matter and bears' digestive tracts do not handle plants well, they must travel to where the most digestible varieties are located. Their memory of such locations is phenomenal. Not only do they remember where they are, but also when the food sources at these places are at their most nutritious.

A bear's solitary existence is, however, disrupted by biological impulses, chief among them mating and rearing young. Female brown bears mate once every three years unless their cubs are killed, which makes them again receptive to mating. Cubs do not leave their mothers until about three years after birth. Female bears are very protective of their offspring, especially from males that would kill and eat them. Hence female bears will seldom take their cubs to places they know male bears frequent.

Mating takes place in early summer, generally between early May and mid-July. As with many bears, implantation is delayed until fall. Birth occurs in the den between January and March. Females with cubs remain in the den longer than males or females without cubs. Bear milk is very thick and rich, higher in fat and protein than the milk of most other animals and its energy content is three times that of human or cow milk. Both brown bears and polar bears nurse their cubs for three years, or until the cubs voluntarily break away from their mother.[23]

The polar bear is the largest of all bears alive today. For the Polar Inuit of northeast Greenland, the polar bear, *U. maritimus*, is *pisingtoog*, the great wanderer. They say that if you follow the bear you will learn much. Barry Lopez in *Arctic Dreams*, explains that curiosity is also incorporated into the term *pisingtoog* – bears wander with curiosity.[24] According to Charles T. Feazel, the polar bear is also called Nanook by many Inuit, 'he who is without shadow'.[25]

As one Arctic scientist remembers with a shudder, the polar bear's sense of smell is extraordinary and they are silent pursuers, especially during a blizzard, when any chance to hear a bear's approach is cut to zero.

Yesterday I watched a bear kill a seal. I shouldn't have . . . The scene was a grim lesson in arctic efficiency. Shuffling along through the snow, the big she-bear looked peaceable enough. Then scenting, through more than two feet of snow cover, a seal's breathing hole in the ice, she froze. The bear shape I'd seen moving against a backdrop of white disappeared in the invisibility of ultimate camouflage. Suddenly, rearing up on her hind legs, she towered, motionless, a silent, menacing apparition almost eight feet tall. She waited. Then, with a dive so fast that the eye couldn't follow, she plunged nose first into the snow. A great cloud of white powder exploded into the still air, mercifully obscuring the seal's final agonies. With her massive jaw and thick neck muscles, the bear crushed the seal's skull and lifted its 150-pound body clear of the water. The power of the upward jerk pulled her prey through the narrow opening in the ice, and broke most of the seal's bones.[26]

The polar bear confounds the many assumptions people hold of it. It is an amazing paradox. A white bear whose skin is black, whose white hair is not white but translucent and hollow and works more efficiently as a solar heat collection system than any system devised by engineers. It is a bear that hunts best while lying down. It is a land animal that swims at speeds up to 6 miles an hour (10 km/h) for long periods of time so that it is often found swimming many miles from either land or ice floes. A thick layer of fat or blubber, especially in the rump area, keeps the bear warm and helps it to stay afloat when swimming. It is a bear whose major problem is not keeping warm in the Arctic, but keeping cool! When other bears in North America are hibernating during the winter, the polar bear is at its most active, roaming Arctic ice packs. Although it moves slowly to prevent overheating, it can also move very fast when required. Spurts of up to 25 miles per hour (40 km/h) on feet the size of large dinner plates are not unusual. It can also leap 8 feet (2.5 m) into the air from a swimming start. Despite its bulk, it can move as silently as falling snow. With its great strength, a polar bear can flip a 200 lb seal into the air. Its stomach can hold 150 lb of fat, which it turns into insulating blubber and energy.

Like other bears, polar bears mate in late spring. They are also characterized by delayed implantation. The fertilized egg does not attach to the uterus wall until around September or October. Cubs are born from late November to early January, and emerge from the den in March or early April.

It is believed that polar bears evolved from a group of light-coloured brown bears isolated in a region of Siberia about 400,000 years ago. From here they spread out to encircle the edge of the Arctic. Polar bears are found in Siberia, northwest and northern Alaska, northern Canada, Greenland and the Svalbard archipelago above continental Norway. Their world is where land and water meet. There are three major breeding groups identified by geographical region: Svalbard-Greenland, northwest Alaska and the Canadian Arctic.

Polar bears evolved distinctive anatomical features and lifestyle. They seldom drink water, mostly because there is so little fresh water around. They could eat snow to quench their thirst but this is not very economical and so they have developed a system that requires them to drink little water. The water they need to process body wastes is obtained by breaking down the fats they digest. Since water is needed to flush out poisons from protein, polar bears mostly eat the fat from the seals they catch, leaving the meat for scavengers. Hence, they reduce the amount of protein in their diets. Their kidneys work in a special way, being adept at removing salts from blood and concentrating it in urine. In this way wastes are reduced.

Polar bears have also evolved a more streamlined physical form for swimming than other bears. To start with, they are lankier in build. A polar bear may weigh from 1,780 to 2,000 lb (810 to 910 kg), and stand 12 feet (3.5 m) tall on its hind legs. Its feet are much larger than those of other bears, making efficient paddles in water and snowshoes on land. It also has small papillae and vacuoles on the pads of its feet to prevent slipping on ice. Polar bears' skulls are smaller and more flattened than those of brown bears and they have more elongated necks, making them more streamlined when swimming and less obvious when stalking seals across the ice or waiting at their air holes. Polar bears' narrower shoulders and chests make them better at slicing through water. Excellent swimmers, polar bears use only their front legs to paddle, while their back legs serve as rudders. Unlike other bears, primarily omnivores with large grinding back molars, polar bears' back molars are reduced in size. But they do have well-developed premolars which they need for slicing and cutting up their largely meat diet.

Male polar bears do not den except for a couple of days and then only to escape an abnormally severe cold spell. Female bears, however, make elaborate dens when pregnant. Only about one third of females mate each year, during a season lasting from March until May. In October or November they dig a den several miles inland. The young are born in December or January after a three-month gestation period and nurse on milk that has the consistency of thick cream. Mothers and cubs emerge from the den in late February, depending on weather and latitude. Cubs remain with their mother for about three years, learning the essentials of hunting and other survival techniques.

Unfortunately, such education is becoming increasingly obsolete. Oil drilling and other extractive technology, industrial trash dumps, toxic wastes, increased settlement of the Arctic region and global warming are all altering the polar bear's world. Lopez has noted that the polar bear is 'a creature of Arctic edges'.[27] The problem today is that both the Arctic and the polar bears are on the edge.

Finally, a bear recently discovered in southeastern Asia may constitute a new and separate species. There is still not enough information on what has been called the golden moon bear. Although there are similarities between this bear and Asian black bears, the new bear is golden brown or, in some cases, blond, and has a light-coloured face. It also has a hint of dark marking around the eyes, suggesting perhaps a connection with pandas or with an early stage in their evolution. It is hoped that by comparing DNA samples of this bear with different Ursidae members, scientists will be able to determine its history and relationship to other bears.

These biographies of the eight known species of Ursidae are drawn primarily from scientific accounts; that is, from what scientists and biologists have seen, measured and analysed. But do such accounts present a complete picture? Lopez and others have made a case for adding the 'truths' of the 'native eye' to the 'truth' of science. As Lopez notes, 'It not only takes a long time of watching the animals before you can say what it is doing; it takes a long time to learn how to watch.'[28] The perspective of science is useful in explaining the chemistry and physics of animal biology and informing a discourse on animal behaviour drawn from limited observation, but what can the 'native eye' tell us? In the eighteenth century, science took over the representation of animals, and the stories derived from those whose daily lives were involved with animals were dismissed as irrelevant.

What have we lost by casting aside these 'native eye' viewpoints? Accounts of human contact with bears are important for painting a larger canvas. Stories, legends and myths are important in telling us not only something about the animals themselves but, more importantly, something about the roles that animals play in people's lives and cultures.

3 The Bear of Legend

On a mountain near Vattis, Switzerland in 1917, workmen digging in a cave made an amazing discovery. Here, in the Drachenloch Cave, prehistorian Emil Bächler reported finding among a jumble of rocks and bones, a limestone 'chest' or 'box' containing a number of cave bear skulls stacked one upon another, all facing in the same direction. Bächler surmised that the 'chest' and the arranged skulls revealed human intent. But what was that intent? Was it part of a prehistoric religious ceremony centred on the cave bear?

Did the cave bear serve as a kind of religious or spiritual force prompting such shrines? Could such arrangements of skulls result naturally? Many prehistorians and paleontologists dispute Bächler's findings and his theory of the existence of an ancient cave bear cult, claiming that there was little contact between early humans and cave bears. Björn Kurtén notes that Bächler contradicts himself in his statements and his drawings of the 'chest' of skulls. Kurtén also points out that there were no photographs of the find, nor was Bächler present at the site when the discovery was unearthed. And, finally, workmen destroyed the so-called 'chest'. Furthermore, Kurtén and others claim that Bächler's find, and the arrangements of bones in other caves suggesting a prehistoric cave bear cult, could be the result of natural action brought about by falling rocks and the displacement of bones by subsequent cave inhabitants.[1]

Opponents of the existence of a cave bear cult also dispute that paintings of bears in French and Spanish caves suggest that bears were of religious significance to prehistoric communities. Kurtén points out that the painted bears are, as best as he can tell, brown bears, a smaller species probably in closer contact with humans than the cave bears that roamed at higher altitudes.[2]

Such reasoning, however, does not convince other prehistorians. László Kordos, among others, feels there is a strong possibility that some spiritual significance was attached to the cave bear by prehistoric humans. In a cave in the Bükk Mountains, he found three cave bear skulls placed in what he believes was an intentional formation.[3] Is this evidence that reverence was attached to the cave bear in Paleolithic times, at least in some places? Could these skulls, so carefully arranged, be the result of some ancient ceremony that honoured the spirit of the cave bear? Recent findings in Belgium of cave bear remains spotted with red ochre suggest that early Neanderthal or other prehistoric people did conduct rites utilizing cave bear bones. How extensive these practices were, however, is unknown.[4]

Long ago bears lumbered into human imaginings and left legends, stories and myths, which gave rise to ceremonies, rites and observances. In the ring of forest, tundra and Arctic coast that encircles the pole in the northern hemisphere, stories and attitudes about bears were remarkably similar in early times, and many of these ancient tales and practices continue today in certain areas. There, bears were respected not only for their strength and physical power but also for their sacred power. Other important attributes deserving of respect were kinship with humans, comprehension of human speech, assuring successful hunts, providing cures, and offering spiritual protection.

In pre-agricultural Finland, bears were honoured as masters of the forest.

Over the millennia, stories told and retold in smoky forest huts spread among cultures in these cold lands of snow and dark forests, permitting people to conceptualize bears, give them meaning and endow them with mystery. The oral tradition passed from one generation to another began to weaken in most parts of the world five or six centuries ago but stories and songs, although fragmented now, remain sources of information for ethnologists and folklorists. They are more than just amusing tales. They are literary sources that offer valuable information on kinship relations and old customs and beliefs. Stories about bears constitute a large percentage of the mythic literature and reveal how people in the past imagined the bear. Some stories have spread thousands of miles in multiple versions and have even crossed from one continent to another. Among the Native Americans, stories were told at night, generally in the winter, across a warming fire or in some ceremonial-defined context. They were didactic, told to

Native American Indians hunting a bear, in a lithograph after the celebrated Western artist George Catlin.

educate children and remind adults of how the world came into being, what the role of the bear was in creation, and what might happen if taboos were ignored or bear hunting rites improperly performed.

The bear was the most powerful animal spirit, and to anger this spirit could prove extremely dangerous. But there was another reason for the extreme respect paid to the bear spirit. As anthropologist A. Irving Hallowell noted, among people in the northern hemisphere, 'the bear was believed to represent, or was under the spiritual control of some supernatural being or power which governed either the potential supply of certain game animals, or the bear spirit alone.'[5] That is, many believed that the spirit of the bear either controlled all the bears or all the animals. The spirit could release them for human consumption or, if angry, hold them back. If the latter, people would starve.

Since bears could understand what humans said, humans were careful not to refer to the bear directly but employed euphemisms to represent it. The Navaho referred to it as 'Fine Young Chief', while among the Koyukon of Alaska it was called the 'Dark Thing'. The Khanty and Mansi of Central Asia used several terms, including 'Swamp Darling', 'Old One of the Forest', 'Darling Old One', and 'Sacred Animal'. The Finns' terms included 'Master of the Forest' and 'Pride of the Woodlands', while the Yukaghir, a people of northern Siberia, refer to the bear as the 'Owner of the Earth'. Common to all is the resonance of spiritual power, strength and control. In ancient Finland, bears were believed to be kind to man unless talked about and called *Karhu*, today the Finnish word for bear. Then they grew angry and brought harm to humans. Apparently bears much preferred to be called 'Grandfather' or 'Forest', since they considered themselves the kings of the

A Finnish bear-head stone club from the second millennium BC, thought to be a weapon with possible ritual uses, reflecting the centrality of bears to pre-historic Finnish culture.

forest. According to the Finns, before man came to the woods there was no creature that dared to defy old 'Forest'. No one dared to call him *Karhu*. He was the forest itself and when he moved the forest moved with him.[6]

For pre-agricultural peoples, the meaning of the bear was rooted in their worldview and their environments. The stories that follow address these worldviews and in so doing give cultural meaning to the bear.

Among the Modoc of California there is a story of the creation of the grizzly bear and of Native Americans and the kinship between the two. It is also a story of the bear as protector and nurturer of humans.

One day, the chief of the sky spirits was walking in the above world and grew annoyed by the cold there. Making a hole in the above world, he pushed all the snow and ice through it until it formed a mountain from the earth below almost to the sky. The chief then stepped through the hole and walked down the mountain. The scene was bleak and devoid of life. Wherever he touched his finger to the mountain a tree sprung up. At one point the chief of the sky spirits picked up a branch and, breaking it into pieces, threw the large pieces into a river at the base of the mountain. There, these large pieces of wood became beavers and the little pieces became fish. From some of the large pieces of the branch, he made grizzly bears. They were large, covered with thick hair, had long, sharp claws and walked around on their hind two legs. The chief of the sky spirits thought they were incredibly ugly and ordered them to live at the bottom of the mountain.

The chief of the sky spirits then looked around and decided he was pleased by the mountain and the world he had created and decided to bring his family down to live in a lodge that he built inside the mountain. The entrance to the lodge was through a hole in the top of the mountain that also served as a smoke hole. One day, when the chief of the sky spirits sat with his family around a roaring fire inside the mountain, the wind spirit blew up a storm. The wind grew so strong that it blew the rising smoke from the fire back into the mountain. This annoyed the chief of the sky spirits, and he asked his little daughter to go to the smoke hole and tell the wind spirit to blow more gently. But the chief also warned his daughter not to put her head out of the smoke hole because the wind might catch her hair and blow her away. She did as instructed but was unable to resist putting her head out of the smoke hole a little way in order to take a look around. That was enough for the wind spirit who, as her father had warned her, grabbed her hair, lifted her out of the smoke hole and tumbled her down over the snow and ice to the bottom of the mountain.

A grizzly bear out hunting found her and carried her home to his wife. The wife, feeling sorry for the little girl, took her in and raised her along with her own cubs. When the little girl grew to womanhood, she married the eldest son of the grizzly bears and in time had many children. When the mother grizzly bear grew old, she began to feel guilty about keeping the daughter of the chief of the sky spirits away from her home in the mountain. She told one of her sons to climb the mountain and tell the chief of the sky spirits that his daughter was alive and where she could be found. The chief of the sky spirits was delighted with the news that his daughter was still living and he hurried down the mountain to see her. He found his daughter living with the grizzly bears and taking care of a brood of strange-looking creatures who he learned were his grandchildren. What he saw greatly angered him. A new race of creatures had been created. In revenge, the chief of the sky spirits cursed all grizzly bears, telling them that from that time forth, they would all walk on four legs and would never be able to talk or use language again. He then took his daughter and carried her back up the mountain and perhaps up into the sky. The strange creatures, half grizzly and half spirit people, travelled far and wide and, according to the Modoc, were the first Native Americans and the ancestors of all the tribes.[7]

In this tale, one learns not only about the creation of grizzly bears and Indians (Indians who tell these tales see themselves as distinct from other peoples), but how similar the first bears were to humans: walking on their hind legs, speaking and living in formal married relationships. They were the progenitors of the tribal peoples of America. To this day, there are some tribes that refuse to eat bear meat since to do so would be to eat their own ancestors. Other tribes have their own creation stories. These generally fall into two types: people emerging out of the earth, or descending from the sky. The Modoc tale is a variation of the sky origin myth, while a tale from the Menominee of Wisconsin, who also see their origin connected to the bear, have the bear emerging from a hole in the earth. The Modoc tale is only one of many Native American creation stories in which the bear figures prominently.

In another bear creation story, the culture hero Väinämöinen sings of the creation of the bear in the great Finnish epic, the *Kalevala*. From a piece of wool thrown on the waters by a female air spirit, the bear is given birth. But the bear is not born at once. The wool is 'lulled' and 'wafted' upon the waters until it is washed ashore. There, Mielikki, the forest mistress and wife of Tapiloa, the lord of the forest, gathers up the wool, lays it in a basket and tends it until the wool is slowly transformed into a bear.

> The Beast grew beautifully
> came up to be most graceful—
> short his leg, buckled his knee
> a chubby smooth-snout
> his head wide and his nose snub
> his fur fair, luxuriant;
> but yet he had no teeth
> nor had his claws been fashioned.

But Mielikki, forest mistress, proclaimed that she would 'fashion claws for him, teeth too . . . if he were to do no harm and get up to no mischief'.[8]

The *Kalevala* relates the birth of the bear from sky and water. The bear has the same origins as the culture hero Väinämöinen, who also achieves form through the agency of a female air spirit, floats upon the water and is later, like the wool that gives birth to the bear, blown to shore. Hence a case could be made that through the stark similarity of their origins, the bear and Väinämöinen are brothers. The bear is intricately coupled to Finnish history and to the Finnish people.

Among the Mansi, a Finno-Ugrian people of Central Asia, the bear originated in heaven. One version holds that the first bear was an unruly son of the sky god, Kores. One day on catching a view of the earth the young bear demanded that his father allow him to visit. Finally, his father acceded to his son's wishes and made a cradle of gold and silver coins suspended on iron chains. On the first two tries, when dropped from heaven, the cradle carrying the bear swung in all directions but did not reach the earth. On the third try the cradle reached earth, landing in the middle of a forest swamp. Before leaving heaven, Kores gave the cub specific instructions: not to touch the sacrificial huts, not to disturb human corpses, and not to harm human beings. He also instructed the cub to eat fruits, especially berries. But the young bear grew bored with life on earth. The summer was hot, with lots of mosquitoes and few berries. The bear destroyed the sacred huts of the people and in winter ravaged frozen corpses in their coffins. Eventually he was killed by hunters who marked the death with ceremonies that allowed the bear's spirit to return to the sky, its proper home.

Important here is the belief in the cyclical nature of the bear's passage, perhaps inspired by its hibernation cycle: it comes from heaven, is killed, and returns to heaven only to come back to earth again.[9] Variations of this tale can be found among the Gilyaks and Ainu peoples of northeastern Asia.

One of the most universal tales – versions are found from North America to Siberia – is the legend of the woman who marries a bear. With such an extensive geographical range, this tale may be thousands of years old. This version is drawn from the Haida culture of British Columbia. The story relates how a group of women encountered bear droppings at a place where they went to pick berries. Ignoring warnings that it was

Winter Sleep by Finnish artist Helena Junttila echoes many folkloric stories of bear–human couplings.

taboo for women to step over such droppings, one young woman not only stepped over them but on them and kicked them. At the same time she hurled insults at bears and mocked them in derisive language. In the afternoon, when her friends returned home, the young woman decided to remain a while longer, having discovered a bush laden with berries (other versions have her spilling her basket of berries and having to pick them up, thus preventing her from returning to the village with her friends). As she picked, she noticed a handsome young man approaching wearing a bear skin cloak. He offered to help her pick berries and told her of other bushes with even more berries further up the mountain. He suggested that they pick them and he would walk her back to her village. It soon grew dark and the young man said it was too late to return to her village and suggested that they should make a camp and return to the village the next day.

On the following day, as they continued to pick berries, the young man used his shamanistic power to make the woman forget about going home. Days turned into weeks as the man led the woman further and further from her village to pick more berries. Finally, when summer passed into fall and it began

left A Tlingit bear mask, from the Pacific north-west of Canada.

right Haida tunic with bear motifs comprising shells and shark teeth, from the Pacific north-west of Canada.

to grow cold, the man decided he would dig a den, and the woman's suspicions that he was actually a bear were confirmed.

That winter the woman gave birth to two children, half human and half bear. In early spring her husband awoke suddenly from his sleep of hibernation and announced that someone was coming. The woman knew that her brothers were searching for her. Several times her husband awoke and each time he said, 'They are getting closer.' Then her husband said, 'They are almost here; I will put in my teeth and kill them.' The woman pleaded with him, telling him that what he heard were her brothers coming to find her and she begged her husband not to kill them but to let her brothers kill him

Encounter (2001) by Helena Juntilla evokes northern European stories of women's relationships with bears.

A Haida carving
of a mother
nursing a bear
cub.

for the sake of their children. He finally agreed but told the woman that upon his death certain rites were to be performed and songs sung.

After her husband, the bear, was killed and the rites performed and the songs sung, the woman, with her two half-bear, half-human children, returned with her brothers to the village. Fearful of turning into a bear herself, she refused to enter into games with them that involved wearing a bear's skin and pretending to be a bear. But in defiance of her wishes, one brother threw a bear skin over her and her two children. As she had feared, she and the children immediately turned into bears. She then killed her brothers and returned to the woods with her cubs.[10]

This story, like most tales, can be interpreted at various levels. Most obvious is the lesson that, if taboos are broken, social order breaks down and disaster follows. At another level, it is a story about anger and revenge, the bear's ability to change shape, to communicate in human speech, and to interbreed with humans. It is this last power that instigated fear and anxiety among women in the northern hemisphere, causing them – at least the unmarried women – to maintain a safe distance from dead bears brought in from the hunt. Women were also not allowed to eat meat from the front of the bear, only from the rump. The reason, according to some stories, is that it is the front side or front legs that do the embracing.

An early tale from Scandinavia, recorded in 1555 by the Archbishop of Uppsala, Olaus Magnus, in his *Description of the Northern Peoples*, told of a beautiful young girl abducted by a bear and taken to his cave. Although he stole her to 'tear her to pieces', he soon fell in love with her and 'he now altered his designs on her to purposes of wicked lust. He immediately turned from robber to lover, and dispelled his hunger in inter-

course, compensating for a raging appetite with the satisfaction of his desires.' To encourage the girl's affections he robbed local farms and brought her fruits and other food 'spattered with blood'. Eventually, the farmers of the region tired of the bear's stealing, found his cave, and killed him with dogs and spears. The pregnant woman was now free but, 'Nature working with two different materials palliated the unseemliness of the union by making the bear's seed suitable. The girl gave birth normally but to a marvel among offspring, lending human features to this wild stock.' The child, a boy, while looking human, had the wildness and strength of the bear and slew those who had killed his father. From this boy descended King Sven of Denmark and a long line of Danish kings.[11]

There are many tales throughout the northern hemisphere of women abducted by bears and forced to serve as wives and

Helena Junttila's painting *Bear Lisa* (1999) gives the bear a gentler face.

Another gentle
bear, this time
in California.

beget children. Sometimes this has political and/or social consequences as the progeny serve as the origin of a lineage or
clan. In some tales, males are abducted and forced to serve as
husbands. In parts of South America there are legends of spectacled bears stealing both virgin girls and unmarried boys. The
long cross-cultural obsession with women and bears is curious

and continues to this day. In many parts of the world women are sexually identified with bears. Some even describe themselves as 'bear women' who have descended from bears in the same way as certain aristocratic families in the past claimed their own origins.

Bears did not always prey upon humans. Sometimes they were exploited by humans, as in this Inuit story from Greenland.

Once, an old couple beyond childbearing age wished for a son. One day the man killed a polar bear and sang a song to it, pleading it to come back to life and be his son. Out of the blood flowing from the dead bear emerged a bear cub. The couple were happy and raised it as their own. When the bear-son grew older, it hunted for the old couple, bringing them harbour seals, ringed seals and other meat. They were happy to have such a good hunter as a son. Then one day the old man asked his bear-son to bring back the meat of an ice or polar bear. Although the bear-son refused, since he did not want to kill his relatives, the old man insisted. Finally the bear-son, out of a strong sense of duty, went forth and later returned with the

A Cherokee bear mask from the southeastern United States.

body of a large she-bear, but when the old couple sat down and began to eat the bear meat, he walked out, never to return. The old couple, left without their bear-son to hunt for them, soon died.[12] Here again the strong kinship connection between bears and humans is demonstrated and also the moral that abusing that kinship relationship can result in tragedy.

For many people around the northern rim, bears possessed remarkable powers: not only could they change shape, they could also come back to life. Perhaps the bears' emergence from their dens in the spring after a winter under ground came to symbolize this resurrection ability. The following tale from the Cherokee of the southeastern United States speaks of this life-renewing capability.

One day a hunter chanced upon a bear and shot an arrow into it. The bear began to run and the hunter gave chase, all the while shooting him with more arrows. Eventually the bear stopped and, pulling the arrows from his body, confronted the hunter, saying: 'It is no use for you to shoot arrows into me; you cannot kill me. Let us go to my home and we will live together.' The hunter grew frightened, thinking that if he did so perhaps the bear would kill him. The bear, however, read the hunter's thoughts and assured him he would be in no danger. The hunter's next thoughts were of food and what he would eat, for he was very hungry. Again, the bear read the hunter's thoughts and told him that he had plenty of food and that the hunter was welcome to it.

So the hunter followed the bear and eventually arrived at his cave. Once inside, the man again thought about his hunger. The bear responded by rubbing his belly and producing nuts, berries and acorns, which the hunter ate until he was full.

The hunter and the bear lived together for nearly a year when suddenly, to the hunter's surprise, the bear said that people from a nearby village would soon come and kill him. He

A Cherokee wood carving of bears and cubs in the wild.

also told the man that after they had done this they would skin him and chop him into pieces. The bear asked the hunter first to cover his blood with leaves and then, as he was being led away back to his village, to look back.

In a few days, as the bear had prophesied, men came with dogs, found the cave and called for the bear to come out. When he did, he was killed, skinned, and chopped into pieces to be taken back to the village. As this was being done, the dogs continued to bark and the hunters thought there must be another bear in the cave. They soon discovered a man inside and recognized him as the person who had disappeared from the village the year before. But before leaving the man did as the bear had requested: he covered the blood with dry leaves. As the man left for the village with the hunters, he turned to look back and saw the bear rise up from the leaves, shake them off and walk slowly back into the woods.[13]

The Mansi of central Siberia also tell a story of transformation, but this time about a human becoming a bear. A young boy was lost in the woods. As he sat on a tree stump wishing to return home, he cried, 'Where shall I see the kin begotten of my father, the kin born of my mother?' At this moment he tumbled from the stump and upon getting up discovered he had turned into a bear. The transformation gave him new confidence and he sang: 'Upon the heath I am the true-born son of the goddess who dwells on the heath down in the forest. I am the true-born son of the goddess who dwells in the forests; I am one who lives by his own will.' In a fit of hubris, he proclaimed he would take whatever God had not granted him.

The Samoyeds and the Lapps also told stories of metamorphoses but, as we shall see later, they 'also practised rites believed to change themselves, or others, into a bear or to change a bear into a man.'[14]

The powers of the legendary bear, however, were greater than warding off arrows and reincarnation. They also extended to curing. Among the Lakota (Sioux) Indians, when effecting cures, 'bear doctors' would sing, 'My paw is sacred, the herbs are everywhere. My paw is sacred, all things are sacred.'[15] The Native American 'pharmacopoeia' was replete with plants they derived from watching bears collect herbs, berries and roots. According to many tribal accounts, one only had to watch what the bear ate to learn what plants were beneficial to human health. Among several of the California tribes, a group of shamans also known as bear doctors were highly respected as healers. They allegedly received their healing powers from bears. The following tale from the Hupa Indians of California is only one story of bears' medicinal powers.

One day, while walking in the world, a bear became pregnant. The more she walked the fatter she became and soon she was too fat to walk. At this point she began to consider her position and wondered if Indians also got in this way; that is, pregnant. Suddenly, from behind her, she heard a voice saying, 'Put me in your mouth; you are in this condition for

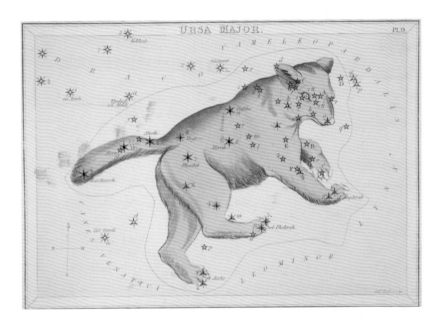

'Ursa Major'
(the Great Bear),
a hand-coloured
etching from
Aspin's 1825
*Familiar Treatise
on Astronomy*.

the sake of the Indians.' When the bear turned round she saw a plant of redwood sorrel. She put the plant in her mouth and the next day she could walk again. So she thought, 'It will be this way in the Indian world with this medicine. This will be my medicine [to them]. At best not many will know about me. I will leave it in the Indian world. They will talk to me with it.'[16]

To some, the bear also held the responsibility for the change of seasons. Since it entered its den in the fall as the days grew short and emerged again in the spring as the days lengthened, it was believed that the bear controlled the sun. The bear that seemingly died in the fall, burying itself under ground when darkness and the cold of winter covered the earth, returned from the underworld in spring bringing the sun and longer days as he once again began to roam the earth.

68

Although not all cultures that honoured bears believed they controlled the sun, many saw the bear as a celestial figure in the night sky. The Great Bear, season after season, slowly circled the Pole Star in a never-ending journey. According to the Mesquakies, or Fox Indians, of the American Midwest, its heavenly travels resulted from a hunting trip gone terribly wrong.

A modern bear effigy from the American Southwest.

Long ago, according to Mesquakie legend, three brothers decided to go on a winter hunt for bears. One brother took his dog along to help in the hunt. Eventually, after walking through woods and brush, they discovered a bear's den. One brother entered it to drive the bear out. He found the sleeping bear and poked it with his bow until the bear awoke and ran outside. The bear managed to elude the brothers waiting outside but they then gave pursuit. The bear ran first to the north and then to the east and then to the west. The brothers looked down and saw the earth far below and shouted that they should turn back. But it was already too late for they were in the sky. To this day, according to the Mesquakie, the brothers and the dog chase the bear around and around the Pole Star. Until they catch the bear, they can never rest.[17]

Like the peoples of North America and Siberia, the ancient Greeks saw the Great Bear prowling the night skies and

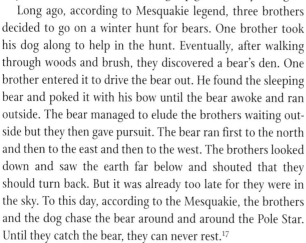

Very early Native American carved stone bear effigies, from Alaska.

attributed its wanderings to the activities of Callisto and Zeus. Callisto, the daughter of Lycon, King of Arcadia, the place of the bear people, was one of the young women who attended Artemis, the protector of wild things and children. One day, Artemis discovered that Callisto was pregnant and as a punishment turned her into a bear and expelled her into the heavens. Another version of Callisto's downfall centres on Zeus. Hera, the wife of Zeus, angry that Zeus had made Callisto pregnant, turned her into a bear after her son was born. When the son, Arcas, grew up, Hera sought to have him kill the bear that was his mother. But Zeus intervened, snatching Callisto away and placing her among the stars as the constellation Great Bear or Ursa Major.[18]

In the lands of forests and lakes and in the Arctic where cold winds sweep over ice packs and tundra, bear legends depicted them as sacred, strong and possessed of powerful medicine. Of all animals in the north, the bear was the most human. Bears were respected partly because of their kinship with humans and also because they were feared. The bear held important knowledge and could bestow blessings or wreak tragedy.

As hunter-gatherers gave way to agriculturalists, the image of the bear in stories changed. Of course, in pre-agricultural times, narrators often took liberties in presenting tales. Depending on the context in which the tale was told, or the creative nature of the storyteller, the story might alter slightly but the symbolic meaning of the bear remained constant. This all changed, however, in a new world devoted to herding and agriculture. The bear became seen as an impediment to progress and was desacralized, made to represent an ogre or a fool, and marked for destruction.

Bears were turned into stupid, menacing brutes or threats to agricultural life. According to Olaus Magnus, bears enjoyed music so much that they terrorized shepherds, often carrying them off after being attracted by the music shepherds played on their pipes. Blowing horns, however, forced the bears to release their victims, for the noise annoyed them and sent them running off back into the woods.[19]

One can find similar stories of outwitting bears in Russian folk tales such as 'The Peasant and the Bear' and 'The Bear and the Cock', where the bear is played for a fool. In more recent children's stories, some of which have tenuous roots in earlier folk tales, the bear is depicted as a clown, a simple, good-natured figure such as Baloo in Rudyard Kipling's *Jungle Book,* or else a vengeful creature as in early versions of *The Three Bears*, where an intruder breaks into the home of the three bears, eats porridge and sleeps in a bed. In one version, the intruder is an old woman whom the bears catch. They attempt to kill her by burning and drowning. When these fail they throw her up in the air where she becomes impaled on the steeple of St Paul's Cathedral. In the more popular version, *Goldilocks and the Three Bears*, the bears discover a little girl in the house and although they chase her, she escapes their wrath. Even Leo Tolstoy's version of *The Three Bears* carries this vengeful element when the small bear that catches the girl sleeping in his bed chases her with the intent of inflicting punishment.[20] Post-agricultural tales generally represented bears in negative terms that applauded their disappearance. It is only now, when bears are marginalized and pose no threat to common daily life, that they have been invested with a gentler demeanour.

Stories help us to understand the world and our place in it; they help us to imagine ourselves. According to some scholars, the stories, ceremonies and rites relating to bears 'allowed the community to see the coherence of its central economic, social and religious values and to reaffirm their significance'.[21] The French anthropologist Claude Lévi-Strauss once observed that animals are good to think with.

The cover
(*c.* 1910) of one
of the many
early versions of
the story of *The
Three Bears*.

The ancient Greeks believed that bears were born form-less and the mother licked them into shape – not unlike the role of education in human society. Stories served to shape bears' relationship to humans, giving them not only meaning in the world but a history, too. Across the northern hemi-sphere, the world of most of the Ursidae family, stories of the 'Dark One', the 'Owner of the World' and the 'Wandering One' were told.

A mother bear licking her new-born into shape, from a 12th-century bestiary.

As we have seen, stories across vast distances were remarkably similar. Is this because of the similarity of environments or because the human mind grapples in similar ways to explain the behaviour and characteristics of bears? Or does it indicate that at some time in the human past the cultures out of which these stories emerged were connected, over time drifted apart yet carried the stories and the archetypical bear along with them as cultural baggage, as Hallowell suggests? As with so many questions about these wonderful animals, we may never know.

4 Bears and Humans

Recently in Finland, a man out picking blueberries looked up to see a female bear with two cubs wander into the clearing. Frightened, he immediately froze, then cautiously backed away and stood by a tree. The bear slowly approached, sniffed him up and down and then licked his face before moving on. Many Native Americans and perhaps some ancient Finns, too, would have seen in this incident a kind of spiritual encounter; an expression of kinship. The man's reaction, however, was to go for his gun. Fortunately for the bear, the man, after finding his gun, could not find the bear. Yet the incident, although ending well for both man and bear, prompted Finnish hunting groups to call for an extended bear-hunting season in order to teach them to fear humans. Bears, however, have already learned to fear humans and, as many bear watchers believe, seldom attack unless they feel threatened, are extremely hungry, or are protecting cubs.

Humans and bears have walked together out of history. We were together in those caves in southern France and in Spain. Over the centuries we have dined on each other. Until the agricultural revolution, our need for the bear was greater than the bear's need for us. Humans have called on bears for warmth, food, medicine, power and protection. An aura of sexual attraction between humans and bears has long existed in legends, as we have seen. In Egypt, it is related that a great white bear prowled the court of Ptolemy II (285–246 BC). 'On special occasions the beast was paraded through the streets of Alexandria, preceded by young men who carried a 180 foot phallus.'[1] Humans have used bears as the symbolic roots of their lineages and clans and to communicate with gods.

Only in a few cultures are bears still seen as kin or as spiritual entities with special bonds to humans or semi-sacred creatures who possess great powers. Now, devoid of their sacredness, most societies regard them as objects in a crowded human landscape or as a potentially dangerous nuisance, to be controlled or exploited for human ends.

The shift came, as suggested in the last chapter, when humans ceased being hunters and gatherers and became herders and farmers. Yet the transition must have been gradual, helped along by the growing influence of the Christian Church in northern Europe. In Greece, bears were said to be the most mysterious of all the wild creatures and it seems they possessed a sacred status. In Rome, they were exploited for entertainment and sport in the Colosseum. Once the Roman armies had conquered the Alps, they turned their attention to the Germanic tribes. In between battles, a growing trade in bears sent a steady stream of them into Rome. Many more arrived from Britain (including what is now Scotland), Syria, Greece and, perhaps, northern Africa.[2] Some became pets, some found their way into private menageries, while others were forced to participate in bloody entertainments for the delight of a gleeful Roman public.[3] Here bears were pitted against lions, bulls and even men. The Emperor Caligula (AD 12–41), for example, had 400 bears killed in a single day in combat with gladiators and other animals. Other Roman emperors treated the populace to similar spectacles, beginning as early as 168 BC.[4]

Bears represented power; a raw force. In Scandinavia and throughout the north ancient legends and customs lingered, and the transition to a new representation took longer than in southern Europe. Among the Finno-Ugrian people the bear was half-human. Even today among the Mansi and Khanty, a Finno-Ugrian people of Central Asia, the bear is an important animal that exhibits human traits, including the consumption of a wide variety of foods, the ability to walk upright, masturbation, similarity of faeces, footprint, physical shape, facial expression and tears.[5] Among the Finns and Lapps, the killing of a bear entailed several days of intricate ceremonies. 'Of all animals the bear was the object of greatest veneration.' It was their 'totemistic ancestor', 'the son of the sky god'.[6] For the Khanty and Mansi, the bear's proper home was the sky but it frequently visited the earth.[7] To swear on the bear or to take a 'bear oath' was the most powerful and binding oath of all.

This reliance on ancient legends is seen in an account written by Pehr Fjellström, a priest in northern Sweden in 1755, who described a Lapp bear hunt. The Lapps traced a bear to its winter den and then, by means of dogs, smoke and flooding, forced it out. Although the process was cruel, the Lapps maintained a profound respect for the animal. Upon returning with the dead bear, several rites were performed. Its skin was saved, the meat was completely used and the bones, after arranging them as in life, were buried. The hunters were prohibited from sleeping with their wives for several days after the hunt and the women could only view their husbands through rings and bracelets. To do otherwise would anger the bear and jeopardize future hunts.[8]

An account from Greenland, dated around 950 AD, records how a great white bear ravaged a village near the home of Eric the Red, the famed founder of the Greenland Norse community. Finally the bear was killed and its meat divided among a rejoic-

ing population. Only Eric the Red expressed remorse, not for the killing of the bear or the distribution of the meat, but because the bear was killed without the old ceremonies.[9] Within the last hundred years, hunters in Finland, Siberia and among the Ainu in Japan were solicitous of bears and extremely careful about how their actions would be interpreted by those they killed. The Finns and the Siberian Ostyak tribesmen, who live east of the Urals, would not only address the bear and give thanks but would attempt to blame the killing of the bear on someone else. Both the Finns and Ostyaks would tell the bear that Russians had killed it so as not to implicate themselves. As among many Native American tribes, people in Scandinavia and Siberia held the belief that bears, even though they appeared dead, remained conscious of what went on around them for hours and perhaps even days after they had been killed.[10]

Vikings held the bear in high esteem as a powerful, unstoppable force. So potent was the bear's spirit that waving a bear skin in battle guaranteed protection. Some Norsemen took to wrapping themselves in bear shirts or skins in the belief that the bear's power and strength would flow into them during battle. Such warriors, called berserkers (from *ber* 'bear' and *serkr* 'shirt'), were particularly feared by the enemy. Some believed that at critical moments in battle such warriors became 'shape-

For the Ainu, the aboriginal inhabitants of Japan, the bear was still of vital importance, and the bear hunt a matter for ritual and ceremony. A 19th-century handscroll, Local *Customs of the Ainu*, shows scenes from 'Iyomante', the Ainu bear ceremony.

shifters' and actually turned themselves into bears. In Old Norse sagas, warriors sometimes engaged in *hamfarir* or shape journeys, sending their spirits in the shape of an animal, generally a bear, to fight in their place. Norwegians used to believe that Lapps and Finns, at moments of great rage, turned themselves into bears. In other accounts, it sufficed to have a bear painted on one's helmet or shield to evoke the spirit and power of the bear. In England, because of the bear's power, 'It was a common practice for aristocratic families in the tenth and eleventh centuries to trace their lineage to bears, as did the earl of Siward, the earl of Kent, Guy of Warwick and the earl of Leicester. Indeed, King Arthur, the leader of the Knights of the Round Table, is connected by name to the bear. Arthur in Latin is *Arcturus*, 'bear'. Svend Estridsen, the eleventh-century king of Denmark, also marked his descent from a bear.[11]

As agricultural pursuits took hold in Europe and spread north, the bears' forest domain was cut down and their symbolic power ebbed. The growing influence of the Church chipped away at their spiritual reputation. Some have pointed to God's injunction to Adam and Eve to 'go forth and multiply' and 'have dominion over all the creatures of the earth, air, and sea' as the inspiration for the Church to 'desacralize' animals. Recent scholarship, however, has cast doubt on this, noting, 'More important was the church fathers' desire to reject classical Greek and Roman ideas.' In an attempt to separate Christians from pagan beliefs and establish a new identity for them, early Church Fathers repudiated the 'classical view' that saw humans and animals as closely related.[12]

During the Middle Ages, with prodding from the Church, the belief developed that animals had a fixed nature and no amount of training could alter that fact. Thus animals could serve as didactic symbols in paintings, sculptures and wood carvings. In

A 14th-century English carved-bear misericord from St Hugh's Choir, Lincoln Cathedral.

medieval churches, animal images were often used to drive home moral lessons or illustrate character traits – the cunning fox, the brave lion, the voracious wolf and the strong but stupid bear. The bear, of course, could be raised to extreme violence but preferred to spend its time sleeping. Often in the misericords, carved into the bottom of medieval choir stall seats, the bear appears stupid or just waking up. The image is of a creature of great strength but also of sloth and clumsiness.

When it came to representing bears, the Church held contradictory views. The doltish image of the bear did not erase the potential for danger wrapped in that shaggy coat of hair. Aroused, bears still possessed a ferocious nature. Hence, St Ursula (her name signifies 'bear'), acquired her name when she protected her 11,000 virgins with the fury of a bear. Besides Ursula, other saints became associated with bears, gaining their reputations by overpowering the bear's violence with spirituality. St Sergius of Radonezh, reputed to have power over animals, tamed bears through sharing his food with them. St

Gall used bread to tame a bear and taught it to fetch wood for a dwelling. Such holy power is illustrated again in the story of St Korbinian (Corbinian), who, on his way to Rome, lost his pack-horse to a bear attack, whereupon the saint forced the bear to carry the load.[13] This story is also attributed to St Claude. These stories are significant for the laity since they confirm the power of the Church not only to tame bears but also the chaos the wilderness represented. An added moral is that if bears can be made docile by the Church, so can the fearful pagan.

For the Church, the bear exhibited other attributes. St Damian reminded people of the bear's lustfulness when he claimed that Pope Benedict was turned into a bear in the afterlife because of his carnal activities on earth. But if the bear was lustful or fearful, he was also caring and exhibited extreme piety. Indeed, 'the bear is the first animal in Christian tradition to be called "brother", because he cares for those in trouble.'[14]

In other cases, bears became associated with saints by accident. St Blaise became identified with bears because he was the patron saint of Candlemas, a holy day which occurred around the time bears emerged from winter hibernation. In popular belief, the saint and the bear were connected and associated with the beginning of spring. In some parts of eastern Europe, Candlemas was also called Bear's Day.[15]

Although the bear became gentle and devout in the hands of saints, most of the population of medieval Europe, living on the edge of the wilderness, lacked the saints' ability to convert wild bears into passive, obedient creatures. For them, bears remained wild and destructive forces, best exterminated. Paintings depicting bear hunts from the thirteenth to the nineteenth century attest to the threat many believed they posed to society. The same was true in other parts of the world. Holy men may have possessed the power to transform bears into affable fellows but the general population, who had to contend with their destructiveness in gardens, fields, orchards and barnyards, saw bears very differently.

Many of the traits the Church associated with the bear between the twelfth and sixteenth centuries were replicated in the bestiaries, or books of beasts, that circulated widely throughout the Middle Ages and into the Renaissance. The *Physiologus*, forerunner of the medieval bestiaries, originated as early as the second century AD in Alexandria. Later translated from Greek into Latin, it described about 40 animals employed as moral object lessons. The *Physiologus* and later bestiaries, however, were 'never meant to be read as works of natural history' but rather 'interpreted the world in a moral and physical sense in order to introduce its readers to the Christian mysteries'.[16] As one scholar notes, animals were moral entities, each 'bearing a message for the human'.[17]

By the thirteenth century, such books were handsomely produced and very popular among the elite. Their mission was to 'redefine the natural world'.[18] Since most of what those authors wrote was garnered from earlier bestiaries or from oral tales, much of what they said about animals proved wrong. The bear in bestiary manuscript 764, written between 1220 and 1250, in the Bodleian Library, Oxford, is an example. It begins, 'The bear gets its Latin name "Ursus" because it shapes its cubs with its mouth from the Latin word "Orsus". For they are said to give birth to shapeless lumps of flesh, which the mother licks into shape',[19] – just as the Church promoted spiritual shaping.[20] These ideas probably permeated down from the ancient Greeks. The great German cleric and natural historian Albertus Magnus, however, would have none of this nonsense of cubs being licked into shape. In his influential work, *De animalibus*, written around 1260, Magnus states that such ideas began with poets and were untrue.[21]

In another bestiary, in contrast to the lion, whose courage is in its breast and whose strength is in its head, the bear's head is weak and its strength is in its arms and legs. Allegorically, 'the bear signifies the devil, ravager of the flocks of our Lord . . .'.[22] Many bestiaries could not refrain from dwelling upon the lustiness of bears, especially where this pertained to human females. It proved difficult to suppress old pagan ideas of bears abducting young maidens for carnal purposes. In Scandinavia, for example, such stories continued to circulate. Although Olaus Magnus, in 1555, recounted the use of bears because of their strength as draught animals to pull ploughs or turn tread wheels to lift water, he could not resist informing his readers about the young woman who, abducted by a bear and made pregnant by the beast, gave birth to a baby with bear characteristics.[23]

In 1607, when Edward Topsell, a University of Cambridge scholar and cleric, compiled his *History of Four-Footed Beasts* (mostly a translation of parts of the five-volume *Historia Animalium* by the famed Swiss naturalist, Konrad Gesner), he catalogued everything then known about bears. He pointed out that they were 'strong and full of courage' and 'can tear in pieces both oxen and horses'. He then related a story similar to that told by Magnus but this time situated in the mountains of Savoy. Bears were 'of a most venerous and lustful disposition' and one was known 'to have carried a young maid into his den by violence, where in venerous manner he had the carnal use of her body'. To prevent her escape, every day when the bear left the cave, he rolled a huge stone before the cave door. The bears' manner of copulation, according to Topsell, was similar to that of humans, whereby the female lay upon her back and the male mounted her, his stomach against hers. In Topsell's time and even earlier, this seemed to be the most remarkable feature about bears and the one that most set them apart from other animals. Topsell even noted that bears copulate for a long time and if they are both fat, 'they disjoin not themselves again till they are made lean'.[24]

Also according to Topsell, bears moved into dens after mating where, without eating, they grew fat only by sucking their front paws. To be able to sleep through the whole winter, bears were known to eat the herb arum, which enabled them to fall into a deep sleep. Bears were subject to blindness and so they raided bees' nests, where the stings caused them to regain their sight. Topsell cautioned that bears were not easily trained and should not be trusted. Bears, he said, will bury their dead, and reports from many countries claimed 'that children have been nursed by bears'. Bears could also provide aid to those ill or in pain. If a woman in childbirth was having a difficult time one needed only to send a stone or arrow that had killed a bear over the roof of the house she was in to alleviate her symptoms. Furthermore, cripples were relieved of inflammation if the livers of a pig, lamb and bear were dried, mixed together, pounded into a powder and placed in the cripple's shoes. Topsell also noted that certain bear parts were useful to prevent palsy and 'women may go full time' if they made 'amulets of bears' nails and wear them all the time they are with child'.[25] These were representations of bears that issued not from empirical observation but from what we now see as the medieval imagination. Although Topsell was writing at the dawn of the early modern period when many other writers of bestiaries were becoming increasingly interested in natural history as a science, Topsell still wrote in the earlier tradition of religious allegories.

He was by no means alone in his beliefs, however. Many people at this time still related old stories and harboured ancient fears. Dragons lay beyond the city walls, deep in dark mountain caves. Certainly the monsters and dragons that peered down from pillars on church congregations throughout Europe rein-

A Flemish tapestry of the early 15th century showing the pageantry of a bear hunt.

forced this fear. Even as late as 1672, when cave bear skulls larger than those of contemporary bears were found in caves in Hungary, the skulls were often attributed to dragons. Large deposits of cave bear bones – then believed to be dragon bones – discovered in caves in medieval times found their way to apothecaries' shops, where they were ground up for medicines or marketed as unicorn horns.[26]

Pisanello's studies in chalks (1430s) are rare realistic depictions of the bear for the time, being neither allegories nor hunting imagery.

By the Christian era, according to Barry Sanders, bears disappeared as a 'subject for visual arts . . . bears no longer inspired the visual or plastic arts to any extent.'[27] The bear began retreating along with the woods that had previously covered much of Europe. Yet occasionally they inhabited paintings and tapestries where they were generally the subject of an elaborate hunt.

84

Painting, one of the best media to reflect changing customs, suggests that hunting bears with packs of dogs began in the seventeenth century. In the eighteenth century, paintings depicted bears in desolate wilderness settings beset by dogs and mounted hunters with spears. In *The Naturalists Library xv* (1840), Sir William Jardine lamented that great hunts with packs of dogs were no longer held in Germany and Poland:

> Formerly . . . a bear hunt was reckoned among the most princely of sports. Hunters on horseback, armed with spears, others on foot, with special weapons, packs of hounds, sustained by numerous couples of bear dogs and mastiffs, and whole troops of country people, some bringing nets of great length, others implements to make fires, and all furnished with horns, trumpets, drums and other kinds of noisy instruments, assembled to drive the game together, and destroy it by open force.[28]

The use of specially trained dogs to hunt bears continues to the present day in many parts of the world.

In America, as in Europe, bears were creatures to be disposed of as quickly as possible. Fur trappers would sometimes trap bears, but there was little profit to be had from their pelts. Professional hunters with dogs, however, were hired by ranchers to kill bears along with wolves and cougars that preyed on sheep and cattle. One of these professionals, Ben Lilly, who hunted bears in the East Texas hill country before moving to New Mexico to hunt the length of the New Mexico–Arizona border, acquired a great reputation for exterminating bears. Indeed, so efficient were professional hunters that today few bears can be found in the west outside Yellowstone National Park and the Greater Yellowstone System that surrounds it.

A German princeling hunting American grizzlies in the 1830s, in a lithograph by Karl Bodmer.

A 19th-century bear hunt, from *Outing* magazine.

Hunts were less of a team effort in the Orient, if paintings are to be believed. Nineteenth-century Japanese paintings show single warriors attacking bears with swords. Here the emphasis is on the skill and bravery of the warrior rather than, as in European paintings, on the extermination of the bear and, by extension, the wilderness.

By the nineteenth century, fears of bears and dragons had long receded. Bears in the wild had disappeared entirely from

An example of modern Finnish jewellery that draws on ancient Finnish designs for fetishes and protective charms.

much of Europe, remaining only as sources of entertainment or in the form of carved replicas used as fetishes, or as adornments. Carvings that might once have been fetishes or that served some religious function in Scandinavia, were duplicated in jewellery. New kinds of bear paintings emerged less as art than as anthropomorphized cartoons.

In the United States, Thomas Nast used animals as political cartoon figures in the pages of *Harper's Weekly* between 1860 and 1880, but the first to use bears in such a way seems to have been William Holbrook Beard, a painter and member of the National Academy of Design. From the 1860s on, Beard painted a series of pictures of bears mocking human foibles, including 'The Bear and the Foxes', 'Bears on a Bender', 'The Bear's Picnic' and – most famous of all – 'The Bear Dance'. Although considered vulgar by some and satirical by others, they were immensely popular with the public. Beard particularly liked to paint bears in anthropomorphic settings because he thought they 'have a smile that is vaguely a human expression, and is a real indication of humor or fun; they are great jokers'.[29] During the last half of the nineteenth century, the animal cartoon genre grew increasingly popular in America, especially in politics.

The Russian Bear and the British Lion at odds over Central Asia, in a 19th-century political cartoon.

The Bear Dance by William Beard shows how thoroughly bears were domesticated in the popular imagination by the 1870s.

If, by the nineteenth century, bears had become a subject of the visual arts, they were also a significant item for natural historians. Beginning around the end of the twelfth century, there was an explosion of interest in natural history led by such luminaries as Albertus Magnus and Roger Bacon. With the discovery of 'new worlds' in the fifteenth and sixteenth centuries, previously unknown animals and plants were shipped back to Europe, sparking scientific debates over classification and theological controversies that threatened to subvert biblical truth. In the course of the eighteenth century the scientific nomenclature for animals and plants invented by the Swedish physician and naturalist Carolus Linnaeus (Carl von Linné, 1707–1778) was gradually established, the same era in which nation-states were outfitting worldwide voyages of scientific discovery. Throughout this century and the next, museums and scientific societies were founded to promote the work of natural historians, many of whom maintained worldwide networks of correspondents who sent in data from far-flung regions.

An early drawing of a bear, reproduced in Thomas Pennant's *British Zoology* (1761).

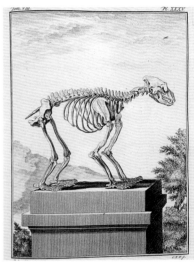

The brown bear as seen in the 18th century, from the Comte de Buffon's *Histoire naturelle* 1759–67).

A bear skeleton, again from de Buffon's *Histoire naturelle*.

First among the British natural historians before Darwin were Thomas Pennant (1726–98), Sir William Jardine (1800–74) and Thomas Bewick (1753–1828). Sprinkled through the pages of their natural histories were illustrations of bears, not only from Europe but other parts of the world as well. Descriptions of their habits, sizes and weights were included, often gathered from older works and from their correspondents' accounts, resulting in a mix of wonderful truths and falsehoods.

With the rise of paleontology in Europe, many were led to the study of prehistoric bears, especially the cave bear. Georges Cuvier's *Recherches sur les ossements fossiles* appeared in France in 1812, while in 1858 the Finnish schoolteacher and amateur paleontologist Alexander von Nordmann published his *Palaeo-azntologie Suedrusslands, I Ursus spelaeus (odessanus)*. In 1833 P.-C. Schmerling brought out *Recherches sur les ossemens fossiles découverts dans les cavernes de la province de Liège*. Others followed.

In more recent times, Björn Kurtén, one of the most prolific students of cave bears, wrote numerous books and articles, including *The Cave Bear Story* (1976), *Pleistocene Mammals of Europe* (1968), T*he Age of Mammals* (1971) and *The Ice Age* (1972), all of which included discussions of prehistoric bears. In 1961 Kurtén's colleagues, F. E. Koby and H. Schaefer, published *Der Höhlenbär*.

In nineteenth-century America, as research on wild animals increased, the study of bears lagged behind. Sportsmen, who, in some cases, wrote quite scientifically, were more interested in deer, elk and moose than they were in bears. And most naturalists hesitated to confront C. Hart Merriam, the leading bear authority of the time. They felt intimidated by Merriam, who, in his exalted position as head of the Bureau of Biological Survey, had the resources of the government at his disposal as well as the status his position afforded. Unfortunately much of Merriam's research turned out to be wrong. A taxonomist, Merriam repeatedly divided the single family *Ursus arctos* into separate species.[30]

Eventually, Merriam's theory collapsed, giving others a chance to move into bear research. The naturalist Ernest Thompson Seton wrote several works on the grizzly, including *The Biography of a Grizzly* (1899) and *Monarch, the Big Bear of Tallac* (1904). William Wright wrote *The Grizzly Bear* (1909) and *Ben, the Black Bear* (1909). A decade later Enos Mills penned *The Grizzly*. Another well-known writer about bears was Theodore Roosevelt, twenty-sixth president of the United States and founding member of the elite organization for hunters, The Boone and Crockett Club, established in 1888. Between 1885 and 1909 Roosevelt published several pieces on bears. He worked in the older tradition, gathering stories from hunters and explorers and conflating them with his own observations as a bear hunter. His writings came to assume the status of 'scientific' truth. Roosevelt began one essay on bear behaviour with the words, 'My own experience with bears

Bears near a hotel in the Yellowstone National Park, Wyoming, c. 1920s.

tends to make me lay special emphasis upon their variation in temper.'[31] He also called for more complete studies of the bears of Yellowstone: 'It is earnestly to be wished that some Boone and Crockett member . . . would devote a month or two, or indeed a whole season, to the serious study of the life history of these bears.'[32]

John and Frank Craighead have done more than Roosevelt could have hoped. They have spent years studying the grizzly bears of Yellowstone and produced articles, research papers and books, making them today's leading authority on the subject. The Craigheads are not alone. Since 1900, perhaps earlier, a growing interest evolved in North America in the preservation of its wilderness and of the plants and animals that constituted much of it. Along with many other animals, bears increasingly became a subject for serious research.

Charles T. Feazel's study of the polar bear, *White Bear: Encounters with the Master of the Arctic Ice*, is the result of years of scientific work in the Arctic. Despite his first-hand accounts of polar bears, Feazel remains wary of them and sees them as the rulers of the Arctic. Kennan Ward's account of grizzlies, *Grizzlies in the Wild*, is less scientific than Feazel's study, but details his observations of bears in one of America's last great wildernesses.

Although there are several studies of pandas, such as the excellent *Men and Pandas* by Ramona and Desmond Morris, George B. Schaller's account, *The Last Panda*, is perhaps the best. Schaller, one of the world's most respected naturalists, based his study on a multiple-year panda project initiated by the Chinese government and the World Wildlife Fund (WWF), and funded in part by the New York Zoological Society. The goals were to investigate panda adaptation to a diet of bamboo, study panda movements, and define conservation methods. *The Last Panda* is also the story of research overseen by two bureaucracies with differing agendas; the Chinese government and the WWF.

Sy Montgomery's *Search for the Golden Moon Bear* is a tale of science and adventure. Montgomery and Gary J. Galbreath travelled throughout southeast Asia to look for this rare creature and to identify cultural practices of bear torture and exploitation in the region. Another scientific but more horrific account, specially researched for the WWF/TRAFFIC, was *The Asian Trade in Bears and Bear Parts* by Judy Mills and Christopher Servheen. Mills has written extensively on the exploitation of bears. Servheen is interested in the international conservation of bears, especially Asian bears and grizzlies.

Findings of bear research remain controversial. The question of the existence of cave bear cults still sparks debates among paleontologists, archaeologists and art historians. Another controversy centres on whether the panda is a bear or a member of the raccoon family, although most scientists now favour the former interpretation.

In the area of behaviour studies, bears still pose problems. Are bears prone to attack humans or are they apt to flee? The rehabilitator Benjamin Kilham, whose *Among the Bears: Raising Orphan Cubs in the Wild*, is one of the best works published on black bear behaviour, believes they are scared of humans and, given the opportunity, prefer to flee rather than attack. Others agree, including Lynn L. Rogers and Jack Becklund, author of *Summers with Bears*. Yet some scientists disagree and fear that those who rely on Kilham when they encounter a bear may discover that the bear has not read his book. Even if Kilham is correct in his observations of black bears, does his thesis hold for other species of bear, such as the polar bear or the grizzly?

Bears pose fascinating questions for science and medicine and their answers could benefit human health. Bears in the northern hemisphere become exceedingly obese before denning, with fat making up much of their weight. Yet the health of hibernating bears is not affected by this fat accumulation. As M. A. Ramsay notes in his article, 'Cycles of Feasting and Fasting', bears 'display some of the most extreme examples of seasonal fatness known amongst mammals and clearly have evolved means of remaining physically fit while obese'. Research seems to indicate that where this fat is stored is more important than the amount stored.[33]

In winter, polar bears add four inches of fat to their hindquarters and lesser amounts elsewhere on their bodies. But this is not the only means by which polar bears keep warm. Scientists are learning much about solar energy from research on these bears, who can often overheat in temperatures way below freezing. What they have found is that the bear's fur 'pulls warmth from one of the coldest places on earth and pipes it more efficiently than steam heat to a skin capable of absorbing it . . . Polar bear skin is, in fact, one of nature's most efficient UV absorbers. Ultraviolet light penetrates clouds, so Nanook's efficient solar collection system works even on overcast days.'[34]

Why after such long periods of inactivity in the den is there no loss of calcium in bears' bones? Why do the bones not become brittle as they do in humans during hospital stays or space flights? It seems bears have the ability to recycle calcium back into calcium bone deposits. Other questions related to hibernation and physical processes remain. How is muscle tone preserved over months of hibernation? Since bears do not eat, drink, urinate or defecate in these periods, how do they avoid ureic poisoning from cellular breakdown which generates the production of urea? Humans recycle about one quarter of the urea they produce back into proteins and the rest is eliminated. Bears apparently recycle all the urea they produce during hibernation. How they do this is still unknown, but the answer might help people afflicted with kidney failure.[35]

Another scientific mystery is the bear's directional ability. After removal from a site, how do bears return unerringly and in almost a straight line to their home ground? As Lynn L. Rogers, a wildlife research biologist with the US Forestry Service, notes, they move 'as if on directional autopilot with little regard for terrain or obstacles'.[36] They almost always travel by night, even on nights that are cloudy or moonless, or during snow storms. Are they guided by scent? Bears have the most highly developed sense of smell of any mammal in North America. Do they possess magnetite – a substance found in the brains of homing pigeons and some other mammals – that acts like a compass? Do they make and store mental maps of areas beyond their home territory? Whatever the process, bears possess a phenomenal navigational system. 'Nuisance' bears removed from national parks, suburbs and farming-ranching areas often find their way back. Often, the return journey is fraught with danger; many bears are killed by cars when they attempt to cross highways at night. Even if the bear does return safely, it stands a better chance of being shot rather than of being caught and taken away again. For some reason, there seems to be more success in removing young bears than older ones.[37]

The impact of modern civilization on bears and their habitats is a serious concern for many interested in bear welfare. In some places suburbs are encroaching upon bear habitats, forcing them into areas where survival is more difficult. Some bears, drawn towards populated areas by garbage, are either shot or removed. The only access most people have to bears is by visiting zoos or national parks. The latter provide the best opportunity for the public to see bears in a natural habitat, but as more people crowd into the parks the bears recede deeper into the interior to avoid human disturbance. Unfortunately, so little is known about bears or their behaviour by people who like to hike, bike and camp in bear country – national parks or wilderness areas – that every year there are confrontations between humans and bears, often resulting in injury or death.

This is especially true in the Arctic, where such confrontations are increasing at a rapid rate. The Inuit, who have shared their world with polar bears for thousands of years, understand and respect Nanook. Many have even claimed to have learned hunting techniques from watching bears. Nonetheless, they observe philosophically that when they hunt the great white bear, sometimes they win and sometimes the bear does. Long years of observation have taught them much about Nanook's behaviour, leading them to disagree at times with scientists who may only observe bears for short periods.

A polar bear looking in through the window of a car, Churchill, Manitoba, Canada, 1997.

The polar bear is still the monarch of the realm of ice and snow. This is what the Inuit know and tourists and oil company workers still have to learn. The polar bear is the only bear that stalks humans. On dark nights in blowing snow or even in the dusk that passes for daylight in the Arctic winter, the white bear

The Kwakwaka'-wakw transformation bear mask of the Kwakiutl Indians of British Columbia, Canada. Mask closed.

The same bear transformation mask, open to show the human within.

is a silent killer – something its victims often learn too late. Despite guards with rifles (who are sometimes called 'bear bait' in jest), hired by oil companies to watch for bears around Arctic oil rigs and to protect scientists studying ice formation and ocean currents, bears still kill or maim those who make mistakes or are ignorant of Nanook's behaviour.

This is also true for tourists seeking a 'bear experience' who ignore posted signs and safety tips in order to get that special photograph. In Churchill, Manitoba, on Hudson Bay where many of Canada's polar bears congregate each summer waiting for the pack ice to start reforming, several businesses cater to tourists seeking to observe bears. Too often, to their misfortune, tourists fail to realize how fast polar bears can run, how high they can reach standing on their hind legs, and how strong they are.

For thousands of years, bears and humans have shared the northern hemisphere. In that time bears have mastered several environments, polar ice fields, mountains and plains in North America, Asia and Europe, and the rainforests of southeast Asia and South America. But because of the exponential growth of human populations worldwide, these environments are being rapidly extinguished along with the bears that live in them. Many organizations and governments are now seeking to prevent the further loss of bears, not least because they are realizing that bears are inexplicably linked to humans and to the human imagination. Or, as some Indian peoples believe – for example, the Kwakiutl of British Columbia – bears and humans are one.

5 The Packaged Bear

In the ninth century, Norsemen risked their lives to hunt polar bears, master killers of the north. Both live bears and their pelts were valuable. What was a bear worth? In 1054 the Icelander Isliefr presented a polar bear to the Holy Roman Emperor, Henry III, and in return was made a bishop. Ten years later, an Icelander named Audun purchased a polar bear during a visit to Greenland. When he presented it to King Svend of Denmark, he was rewarded with a magnificent ring, a pouch of silver, a ship full of cargo and money enough for a pilgrimage. Polar bears were so valuable that, by 1500, Russian tsars maintained a royal monopoly on the trade of bears captured in Russia. Although all bears were prized, the polar bear was the most coveted because of its distant provenance and rarity. Fred Bruemmer notes that they were the ultimate status symbol.[1] It is bears' commercial value – their reprocessing into money-making productions such as status symbols, fighters, dancers, bicycle riders, rollerskaters, musicians, zoo exhibits, trophies, teddy bears and advertising icons; in short, the 'packaging' of bears and the profit made from them – that is explored in this chapter.

Bears were long a marketable item in Rome and in great demand, especially for the Colosseum. Perhaps it was the long shadow Roman civilization cast across Europe with its memories of blood and gore in the arenas that spurred the medieval

In a pan-European practice, tethered bears are attacked by hounds on this 16th-century decorated glassware.

Bear baiting in 17th-century England, from John Brand's 1888 *Observations on Popular Antiquities*.

mind to regard bear baiting – bears tethered to a pole and set upon by dogs – as a popular form of 'entertainment'. The bear's destructive force and power could be used to turn a profit, and in medieval Europe it was. Bear baiting took place in villages and at fairs throughout Europe. The cruelty of the 'sport' seemed to arouse little compassion in the breasts of medieval Europeans. Bear baiting reached England by the eleventh century (some put it earlier), and continued until the eighteenth, but was most popular between 1500 and 1680. In towns and villages, at country wakes and in ale-house yards all across the land, bears tethered to stakes or poles were tormented with sticks, stones, whips, pepper and blinding before they were set upon by dogs. In many cases, to provide the dogs with greater protection, the bears' teeth were knocked out with rocks and they were declawed. Dogs generally attacked the bear's head, ripping off its ears and lacerating its nose and lips. If the bear exhausted the first group of dogs, they were replaced with others until the bear succumbed.[2]

According to historian Keith Thomas, Queen Elizabeth I watched a bear-baiting exhibition in which thirteen bears were killed. Such exhibitions were regarded as appropriate 'for royalty or foreign ambassadors'. In the sixteenth century, London sported many 'bear gardens' where bears were baited, the most popular in Southwark, a rough section of the city that contained the Globe and the Rose and Swan theatres. Some bear gardens were large, tiered structures that could hold up to a thousand spectators. Playhouses alternated between presenting plays and holding bear-baiting exhibitions. Although the Puritans under Oliver Cromwell detested this 'sport', referring to it as a 'filthy, stinking and loathsome game', they made little progress in stopping it. Laws against bear, bull and badger baiting were passed in some parts of England, but it was not until 1835, when Parliament made it illegal, that baiting finally ended. Nevertheless, the 'sport' continued in many other parts of the world.[3]

In Mexico and among California's Spanish inhabitants, pitting bulls against bears proved a popular pastime between 1816 and the 1880s. These spectacles usually took place on Sundays and holidays. Ranchers used wild Spanish bulls, which one observer called 'the noblest game in America'.[4] A bear often killed several bulls before dying.

Today, in parts of Pakistan and other Asian countries, bear baiting remains popular, drawing large weekend crowds. As was the case in England, bears with their teeth and claws removed are set upon by pit bull dogs specially trained to kill. Although the Pakistan government claims to have laws against bear baiting, it does little to stop it, fearing an angry response from rural areas of the country where it has long been tradition.

Native Californians Lassoing a Bear, a colour lithograph of c. 1873.

In medieval Europe, bears were exploited in other forms of 'entertainment'. Forcing bears to dance on their hind legs is an ancient practice that probably began in India, but there is some evidence for it in ancient Rome. Both brown and sloth bears were used, but Asian black bears were preferred because of their apparent ability to remain up on their back feet for long periods of time. Gypsies carried this entertainment to Turkey and then to Europe. Training bears to dance in so-called 'bear academies' began with young cubs taken from the wild after their mothers were killed. Training was accomplished by various means. The most humane was to encourage the cub to stand on its hind legs by holding food above its head. Crueller methods (still used today), included piercing a bear's lip or nose and inserting a ring used to pull the animal up into a

A poster for a bear-baiting event in Pakistan, 1997.

Bear baiting in Pakistan, 1997.

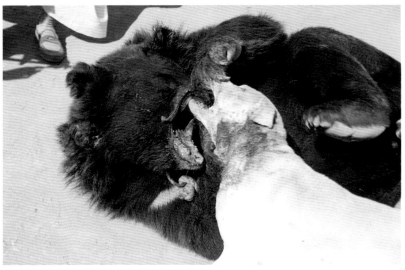

A dancing bear in Bulgaria, 1991.

standing position; drilling a hole through the roof of the bear's mouth and inserting a cord or ring to pull it erect – a method preferred in India; or forcing it to dance on a hot metal plat-form, thereby training it to associate music with burned feet and lift its feet up accordingly.[5] In Magnus' 1555 account, both Russia and Lithuania were famous for their dancing bears. Bears were starved until they were docile, when trainers went among them dressed in bear skins and played musical instru-ments. Eventually bears could be trained to shuffle on their hind feet and even hold bowls for begging.[6] England finally banned dancing bears in 1911. Eventually many other European coun-tries passed similar laws. But they are hard to enforce and in some Balkan and Middle Eastern countries harnessed dancing

Dancing bears in the Auvergne, France, 1905.

bears are still used as tourist attractions,[7] and also often seen in circuses.

Menageries, another commercial use of bears, date back to ancient Egypt and other major cities in the Middle East. The Romans also kept menageries in which bears were exhibited. Before 1800, kings, popes and nobles maintained private zoos on their estates to impress their guests. Given as gifts, bears served

A Hungarian Gypsy with a performing monkey and a dancing bear, Paris, 1962.

to grease the wheels of medieval diplomacy, especially rare polar bears, as we have seen. But brown bears also filled cages and pits. Before 1400, the convent of Saint Gall in Switzerland kept bears and other animals. The Swiss city of Bern had a bear collection as early as 1441, which became better established in 1549, some years before Charles IX of France established his own animal park in Paris in 1570, including bears.[8]

As private menageries gave way to scientific zoological parks and gardens in the eighteenth century, bears continued to serve as major attractions. Although often displayed in pits, they always posed a danger to the public since they were excellent climbers. Still, pits allowed visitors to feed them by means of food attached to sticks. The bears' antics of begging, sitting, climbing and standing on their hind legs amused and delighted the crowds. Despite the dangers pits held for bears and humans alike, they did serve to bring them closer together. In some places, such as Bern, bear pits were not only connected to zoos but could also be found in the city centre. The bear maintains a special place as Bern's official symbol because the city was to be named for the first animal killed on the spot where it would rise – and that animal happened to be a bear. Bears serve a similar official function for the cities of Berlin and Madrid. States and countries have also employed bears as political totems, notably California, known as the Bear Flag state, and Russia.

Bears pose a major problem for zoos because their intelligence and curiosity make them notable escape artists. Still, many zoos are now engaged in the preservation of endangered bears and monitor breeding programmes through International Stud books maintained for each species. This ensures the wide distribution of genetic material and helps to prevent the damaging consequences of inbreeding. These zoo breeding programmes are now the only hope for some bear populations.

But whereas many zoos see themselves as educational institutions seeking to present animals in ways that will better inform the public about 'animal behaviour' and appearance, circuses are just the opposite.

In a different way, circuses did an even better job in 'bridging the gap' between humans and bears. The purpose of circuses since Roman times, and even earlier, has been to entertain. To this end, they distort animal behaviour, forcing them to perform tricks or routines that make them appear ridiculous. Because bears are intelligent, agile, adept at performing repetitive tasks and possess a rather human appearance, they are valuable additions to any circus. They are trained to mimic human behaviour by being taught to roller skate, dance, ride bicycles, walk on stilts or on tightropes, and play musical instruments. The interesting point is that bears have the intelligence and coordination to be able to perform such feats. The 'humour', if there is any, is in how silly – some would say absurd and disrespectful – it is to make bears perform in these ways. Many would claim that such actions insult their natural dignity.

One bear trainer, the colourful James Capen Adams, ('Grizzly' Adams), wandered the American West capturing grizzly bears and 'taming' them with whips and clubs. He beat one female bear into submission before dragging her behind a mule. Eventually he and his 'pet' bears joined P. T. Barnum's early travelling show. During one performance a bear dealt him a blow on the head which pretty much ended his career.[9]

Bears, while popular in the circus, were less appreciated in the fur trade. From the sixteenth to the eighteenth century, furs, especially those from North America, became a major item in the European trade. So much so that the fur trade proved the prime reason for France's claim to Canada. In North America and in Russia the fur trade was an extension of a major industry

Acrobatic bears in the Moscow Circus, 1956.

Cycling circus bears, c. 1878.

centred in Paris and London. Although many American states put bounties on bears that were trapped or shot within their boundaries,[10] they were never a major trade item as were other animals such as beaver, bison, mink, marten, otter, muskrat, fox and raccoon. Bear hides were used as blankets or winter robes on sleighs in Scandinavia and Russia, but were rarely used for this purpose in America and then only on the frontier, where they might substitute for blankets. Bear skins did prove valuable for one item of clothing in England. Beginning in the mid-eighteenth century, they were used for headgear in England as part of the uniform of the Grenadiers, and later the Coldstream, Scots, Welsh and Irish Guards. Before the coronation of Queen Elizabeth II in 1953, thousands of black bears were killed in Canada to make into 'bearskins' for the five elite infantry regiments. In 1968, the Great Bear Hunt took place in Canada, again to supply pelts for Guards' bearskins. This time only 300 pelts were exported. The British military insists that the fur for this headgear comes only from culled Canadian bears, but the Ministry of Defence recently decided to search for a synthetic substitute. Beyond their use for hats, there was otherwise little use for the pelts.[11]

Killing bears for other reasons, however, did reduce bear populations and provide some with an income. For others it served as a ritual for entry into manhood, as in the stories and legends associated with early nineteenth-century American frontier hero, Davy Crockett. During his orgies of frontier killing, Crockett never hesitated to take on a bear. He once bragged that he had killed 105 bears in a single winter and on another occasion, finding a bear and an alligator locked in combat, he killed them both and ate them on the spot.[12]

From the nineteenth century, sportsmen enjoyed hunting bears as trophies, prizing their heads and coats, which were

A soldier in the Scots Guards wearing the traditional 'bearskin'.

memorialized into rugs. Hunters travelled far for the opportunity to kill bears. Under Nicolae Ceauçescu, Romania raised bears for hunting. They were overseen by foresters who were responsible for different districts of the country and who kept track of the bears' weight, size and condition. Killing bears from the cover of a blind, or hide as it called in Romania, seems to have been one of Ceauçescu's greatest pleasures, who would have bears driven to his hide by drummers. In just one day, he killed 24 bears, for which he earned the name among his foresters of the Butcher of

Romania. Foreign hunters can still bag a large bear in Romania for $15,000, exclusive of travel and lodging.[13]

Stories about bears go far back in the mist of time. Because stories and illustrations are politically and ideologically charged, they illuminate specific historical and cultural periods. An example is the epic Anglo-Saxon poem *Beowulf*, perhaps the earliest western European contribution to the genre. Although the story is not directly related to bears, the hero Beowulf's name translates as bear-wolf. Like the ancient tales that claim the bear's left forefoot is stronger than its right, so Beowulf's left arm has the strength of 30 men. Armed with this bear strength and the help of God, Beowulf is able to kill the monster Grendel as well as Grendel's mother and a fire-breathing dragon.

Other stories of a more recent vintage, often expressly for children, like the Scandinavian tale *East of the Sun and West of*

A Polar bear rug in a fantasy Oriental harem, in a 1903 painting by Adolphe Weisz.

the Moon and *Beauty and the Beast* may draw upon ancient legends. They illustrate that in reality things are often not what they seem. The first tale tells of a young woman who marries a white bear to save her family from poverty, but soon discovers her 'husband' is really a man, but one cursed to be a bear by day. She learns learns this by disobeying instructions never to look at him at night; to do so will result in his departure and marriage to a troll hag somewhere 'east of the sun and west of the moon'. The second tale is similar. A young girl marries a beast who has been cursed, usually a bear, in order to save her father. The bear is gentle and kind, subverting its usual image. In both tales the love of the young women is so strong that the curses are lifted, allowing the bears to gain permanent human form. Another story in this genre is the Norwegian folktale *White Bear King, Valemon*, where a woman marries a bear to obtain a golden wreath. As in *East of the Sun and West of the Moon*, he is cursed – this time by a troll hag – to be a bear by day and a man by night.

By the late nineteenth and early twentieth century, stories of animals, including bears, were popular among the general public in the United States. At a time when many Americans were growing alarmed by the disappearance of wildlife, the bear was repackaged to become an important symbol for the wilderness. Ernest Thompson Seton, the nature writer and naturalist, published two major works on bears, *King of the Grizzlies, the Biography of a Grizzly* and *Old Silver Grizzly*. In his books bears narrate the stories. Seton expressed sadness about the bear's fall from grace, the 'king of the wilderness' now so ignominiously reduced in stature. 'The giant has become inoffensive . . . seeking only to be left alone.'[14] The bear had abdicated his kingdom.

Other American writers, such as William Faulkner in his short story 'The Bear' (later expanded in *Go Down, Moses*, 1942),

A Kay Nielsen
illustration to
Thorne-Thomsen's
1914 *East of the
Sun and West of
the Moon.*

An illustration relating to Julia Corner's 1854 play for children *Beauty and the Beast*, by Alfred Crowquill.

BY MISS CORNER AND ALFRED CROWQUILL.

wrote in symbolic terms. Faulkner's bear is less an animal than the symbol of wilderness, and its death foretells the end of the wilderness. In the erotic novel *Bear* by the Canadian writer Marian Engel, the protagonist, a woman named Lou, seeks to have intercourse with a bear only to find him indifferent to her and her sexual needs. Lou learns the futility of projecting her desires on nature and judging nature in human terms.

Bears also appeared in films and photographic works and were treated in much the same way as in literature, only anthropomorphized to a far greater extent. In Walt Disney films, bears are depicted as kind, happy and somewhat stupid, as in the characters of Baloo in *The Jungle Book* and Brer Bear in *The Tales of Uncle Remus*. In the film *Grizzly Falls*, a female grizzly serves as a surrogate mother in its protection of a young boy. But other films, such as *Night of the Grizzly*, *King of the Grizzlies*, *The Edge*, and *Escape to Grizzly Mountain*, to name just a few, stereotype grizzlies as fearsome killers.

Some film-makers, however, have sought to present bears in a better light. *Bears*, a recent film that made the rounds of IMAX theatres, besides exploring some of their rich mythological representations, attempted to portray bears as themselves. A beautiful 1989 film by Jean-Jacques Annaud, *The Bear*, offers a naturalistic live animal account that treats bears in a sensitive manner.

Bears have also been the subject of dozens of 'coffee table' books authored by naturalist photographers. They, too, seek to present the animals in realistic situations, such as hunting, nurturing, fighting, climbing and mating.

As literacy increased and childhood became more defined, at least among some classes in nineteenth-century western Europe and the United States, popular children's stories featuring bears tumbled off the presses. Probably the most famous of all bear tales, *Goldilocks and the Three Bears*, proved innovative in dressing the bears in human clothing and placing them in a house with furniture. This anthropomorphizing of bears would be followed in most children's literature. The tale proved so popular that Leo Tolstoy wrote his own version along with another story entitled *The Bear in the Troika*. Many other Russian writers, including the poet Aleksander Pushkin, wrote stories about bears, some rooted in Russian folklore.

Many humorous 'tall tale' stories like 'A Bear Hunt in Vermont' (1833), 'The Big Bar of Arkansaw' (1841), and T. Hittell's *The Adventures of James Capen Adams, Mountaineer and Bear*

Hunter (1860), entertained the public in the United States. Just as bears highlighted frontiersmen's exaggerations, Rudyard Kipling used Baloo, the bear in *The Jungle Book* (1894) to mock the pretensions of the Victorian era.[15] Soon a host of other bears joined the ranks of those already in literature. Winnie-the-Pooh, created by A. A. Milne, inhabited the Hundred Acre Wood along with his owner, Christopher Robin, and his other animal friends, while Paddington Bear, according to his creator, Michael Bond, was found in London's Paddington area, having survived a perilous trip from Peru. Seymore Eaton's Roosevelt Bears romped through the pages of several books, meeting famous people in different countries and dressing up in national costumes. Other bears like Teddy Brighteyes, Big Teddy and Little Teddy, Rupert Bear and Sooty delighted English children, while Mishka in Russia, Billy Bluegum in Australia, Mr Bear in Japan, Bussi Bar in Germany and many cartoon bears did the same for children in other lands.

As much of the American wilderness slid into memory, so too did the wild bear, to be replaced by 'packaged' bears in zoos, museum dioramas, paintings, cartoons, songs, toys and advertising. In the late nineteenth and twentieth centuries, bears were increasingly anthropomorphized, not only in literature but in western culture as well. Bears' 'animal' aspects were sloughed off; their roars, their threatening teeth and claws, their impressive bulk and power. Through the power of packaging, bears instead took on roles that human cultures assigned to them. The new image engendered a vision of bears as fuzzy creatures with rotund bodies suggestive more of fat than muscle, walking on hind legs, speaking European languages, and possessing a foreshortened humanoid face with a smiling demeanour and expressive eyes.

In 2002, the US Postal Service issued a stamp commemorating the hundredth anniversary of the teddy bear. It marked

Early versions of *The Three Bears* often omitted Goldilocks, the modern focus of the story. This illustration dates from 1888.

THE BEAR, WITH HIS WIFE AND SON, TAKES A WALK.

The original Winnie the Pooh with some of his animal friends.

US postage stamps honour the centenary of the teddy bear.

perhaps the most famous packaging of bears in history. The teddy bear story begins in Mississippi with President Theodore Roosevelt. Bears were one of Roosevelt's passions. In November 1902 an incident took place that would forever link Roosevelt's name with bears. Roosevelt accepted a friend's invitation to take part in a bear hunt. For five days, as they tramped through the hot Mississippi Delta country, the hunt yielded no bears but a great deal of frustration. Roosevelt was annoyed when he failed to get a shot off at the only bear 'raised'. Finally his luck turned; the dogs had located another bear. His hosts, anxious that he should shoot a bear, sent hunters scattering off through the cane breaks to track the animal down. When the dogs eventually surrounded the exhausted animal, it was stunned and roped to a tree. Informed of the capture, Roosevelt hurried to the spot, but upon seeing the helpless, gaunt and bloodstained black bear, he refused to shoot it.[16]

Although this is probably the true story of what happened, two other versions gradually emerged. One told of a young bear, hardly more than a cub, tied by a rope to a tree that found itself before the great hunter. Roosevelt, priding himself as sportsman, refused to shoot so young a bear, especially one bound by ropes. The other version, written many years later by one of the reporters on the trip, claimed that the bear was an old female, weighing only 235 pounds and lame with arthritis. When

Roosevelt arrived, she was tied fast to a tree with ropes and surrounded by dogs. As in the earlier version, Roosevelt refused to shoot the sad and decrepit animal as unsportsmanlike. The first 'substitute' story, the tale of a president who refused to kill a baby bear, caught the public's fancy and inspired artist Clifford Berryman's whimsical cartoon showing a very Victorian Roosevelt sternly refusing to shoot the bear cub.

The story and the cartoon attracted the attention of Russian-born Morris Michtom, a novelty store owner in Brooklyn. Growing up in Russia, Michtom was well versed in folk tales about Mishka, the famous Russian bear. Michtom made a couple of stuffed bears and put them in his shop window. They sold immediately. He made more bears and then had the idea of writing to President Roosevelt, asking him if he could use his name on

'Drawing the Line in Mississippi' by Clifford Berryman, the 1902 original 'Teddy' Roosevelt cartoon.

An all-American assembly-line teddy bear, commemorating its centenary.

the bears. Roosevelt wrote back giving his permission (the letter has since been lost), and the Teddy Bear marched into history. By 1907, Michtom had a factory turning out hundreds of teddy bears each year.[17]

About the same time, across the Atlantic in the Black Forest region of Germany, Margarete Steiff also began turning out stuffed plush mohair bears for the toy market.[18] Neither Michtom nor Steiff could keep ahead of the demand. In 1917, 974,000 Steiff bears were produced and were still not enough. Other toy companies were soon turning them out by the thousands. Not only did toy companies make several different models but also changed the models yearly. Variations included different shapes and sizes, the degree of plushiness, moveable arms and legs, and head size. Some bears growled when squeezed, some were put on wheels, while others served as 'rocking horses'. There were also bear games, dishes, mugs, clothing, spoons, pails, tea sets, carts, stuffed mother bears with cubs, sheets and pillow cases.[19]

The teddy bear craze spread swiftly across continents, reaching Australia, Asia and South America. Bears were not gender specific. Both boys and girls received bears as presents. This worried some toy makers, who believed that the rage for bears might threaten the doll trade. Soon, teenagers and even some adults began carrying teddy bears around. Evelyn Waugh, author of *Brideshead Revisited* (1945), had his character, Lord Sebastian Flyte, carry around a stuffed bear named Aloysius during his years as a student at Oxford University. To the surprise of many, the stuffed bear craze kept growing. Bears even became collectibles for adults who formed teddy bear clubs. In 1994, one stuffed bear fancier paid £110,000 at a Christie's auction for Teddy Girl, a Steiff bear made in 1904. There are even teddy bear museums.

Why this sudden craze for bears at the turn of the twentieth century? What was it about bears, or the period, that elicited

A teddy bear picnic in progress.

A satisfied visitor to the London Teddy Bear Museum.

A teddy bear card game.

such an affectionate response from the public? A growing involvement with nature was sweeping over America with the development of national, state and city parks. New forms of urban transportation facilitated suburban development and there was an increase in the number of urban zoos. Psychologically, a growing sense of anxiety that crept in among the population as the industrial age accelerated probably contributed to the acceptance of the teddy bear as a figure of comfort.

But what made them so attractive in other countries? In Philippa Waring's excellent book *In Praise of Teddy Bears*, Waring quotes Colonel Bob Henderson, who claims the teddy bear is an archetypal symbol derived from 'ancient mythology' and deeply rooted in the human subconscious. Teddy bears stir the human imagination, which links the conscious mind to the archetypal symbol in the 'collective unconscious, with the spiritual realm of divine Ideas'. The teddy bear 'functions as a surrogate for the mother as comforter, and for the Holy Ghost as The Comforter'.[20] Perhaps, but this does not explain why some people are passionate bear collectors and others are not. And why do bears excel as comforters while other animals or dolls have a lesser emotional appeal?

The answer may be because teddy bears are more humanoid than other animals. According to psychologist Paul Horton, teddy bears are so similar to the human configuration that they have greater comforting potential: 'The bear is enough like a human for the child to relate to it, but different enough to distinguish it . . . It's ideally situated in psychological space.'[21]

Whatever the real reasons for their attraction, during Christmas seasons teddy bears take over large department stores in many countries. In Germany during the hundredth anniversary of the teddy bear, a large festival was held complete with parades in the town where the Steiff bear was born.

A child takes
Teddy for a spin
in Paris, 1947.

At the time when the teddy bear fad was sweeping the
United States, people not only cuddled teddy bears but also
swayed on the dance floor to the *Polar Bear Polka* (1880), *The
Teddy Bear* (1907), *The Grizzly Bear* (1909), *Kill the Bear* (1912),
The Dance of the Grizzly Bear (1910), *That Society Bear* (1912), *The
Grizzly Bear Rag* (1912) and *The Teddy-Bears' Picnic* (1913). The
dances mostly consisted of stomping steps, imitating bears.

Bears have long been part of architectural detail, often evok-
ing ancestry, strength or power. The peoples of the Northwest
Coast of North America carved bears into totem poles, sometimes attached to their plank houses, serving as an entrance.
Such representations confirmed that the inhabitants of the
house reckoned their descent from bears. Today, sculptured
bears often grace the entrances of buildings or zoos, symboliz-
ing strength, power, national past or a sense of purpose.

Evidence of Berlin's fascination with bears was displayed in the summer of 2001 when dozens of life-sized bears lined the Kurfurstendamm, the city's main tourist area. A competition among local artists to design and paint humorous bears provided visual excitement for both tourists and Berliners.

The popularity of teddy bears was not lost on the advertising industry. Here bears were creatively packaged to sell products. According to Marty Crisp in her book *Teddy Bears in Advertising Art*, teddy bears have been used to promote everything from airlines to appliances and from vacuum cleaners to varnish and video stores. The public endowed teddy bears with a bundle of positive traits, including trustworthiness, loyalty, friendliness, warmth and dependability. With such traits, they made excellent

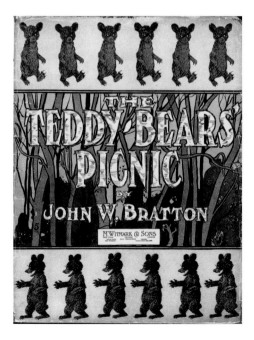

The sheet-music for John W. Bratton's *The Teddy-Bears' Picnic*, 1913.

The bear on the
Finnish Historical
Society building
in Helsinki.

The bear in
front of the
Bloomington
Library in
Indiana.

right: Bears, the
city's mascots,
on the streets of
Berlin in 2001.

cross-cultural sales ambassadors worldwide. According to Crisp, 'Since teddy bears never lie, businesses that use bears as their trademark or as a related promotion can be seen as trustworthy, dependable and concerned about the customer.'[22] Different species of bears lend themselves to the promotion of different products. Crisp notes that whereas 'polar bears represent coolness and freshness or cleanliness and whiteness' and hence are used for soft drinks, mints, liquors, ice cream and soaps, 'grizzlies and black bears represent strength' and are employed wherever an image of toughness and durability is important, such as in clothing, shoes, car batteries, beer, cereals, sports teams and tools. Bear cubs, however, symbolize playfulness, safety and gentleness, making them ideal in promoting children's clothing, foods, candy and motels.[23]

Probably the most famous bear associated with the promotion of a cause is the US Forest Service's Smokey Bear. Smokey started life as a real bear, found as a cub during a forest fire in New Mexico. When he was rescued all four of his paws were severely burned. The firefighters called him Smokey and decided to use him in alerting the public to their role in preventing forest fires, using Smokey's motto: 'Only *you* can stop forest fires.' Throughout the national park system, and in magazines, billboards and on television, Smokey appeared in cartoon form wearing a forest ranger hat, blue ranger pants, and holding a shovel. Only recently has Smokey been 'demoted', as current theory holds that occasional fires are beneficial to forests. The real Smokey ended up in Washington, DC's National Zoo.

About the only area where bears do not project a positive image is in the stock market, where they signal a dropping market. How this came about is a subject of debate. Some explanations seem far-fetched yet may still be true. One is that when a bear seeks something in a tree it pulls it down, whereas

'Fresh and cold – Direct from the North Pole – Lager Beer', c. 1877.

Karhu ('bear') beer.

an attacking bull uses its horns to throw its victim upwards. Another theory holds that the term's origins stem from eighteenth-century England when the saying, 'Don't sell the bear skin before the bear is caught', described those who sold short expecting the market to fall and hence were known as 'bear skin jobbers'. Others cite a 1721 play, *Refusal*, by Colley Cibber, in which a character bemoans his loss on the London Exchange, saying, 'Every shilling, Sir; all out of stocks, tuts, bulls, rams, bears, and bubbles'. Still other theories suggest that the word 'bear' is the verb to bear down or depress and hence to lower the market.[24]

A panda in a 1930s Chinese book illustration.

Finnish bear playing-cards, one item among a myriad of bear marketing.

As the bear was packaged into zoos and circuses, served as a representative figure in art, films and photographs; was snapped up as a toy; engraved on postage stamps; portrayed on playing cards; squeezed between book covers; launched into song and dance; and manipulated in literary metaphors to stand for wilderness or rites of passage, it disappeared as a real biological animal from peoples' lives. Whether the bear will continue its disappearing act, this time literally, is the subject of the next chapter.

This pre-revolutionary Russian silver cigarette case has a bear on one side.

6 Road to Extinction?

It is sad to think that toy stuffed bears outnumber real bears. As toy bears multiply, they fill the comfort needs of a growing human population that is inexorably forcing bears into extinction. The human demographic increase is destroying bear habitats, resulting in fragmentation of bear populations and in a decrease in bear numbers. Today, six, perhaps seven, of the eight species of bears are declining both in numbers and in range.

The brown bear roamed throughout Europe until about the sixteenth century. Until the 'agricultural age', bears and humans, despite sharing an ecological niche, had managed to coexist. But once the human population increased and shepherds and farmers replaced hunters, this niche became overcrowded, setting bears and humans on a collision course. Now bears exist in small, fragmented populations in only the remotest parts of Europe and are likely to disappear altogether if a management plan for their survival is not soon implemented.

Habitat destruction is most severe in the rainforest areas of South America and Southeast Asia, and in parts of the Arctic. Rainforest loss is only partly due to large lumber corporations that build roads into the forest to clear cut trees. Such activity allows the landless poor to move in and collect wood for fuel or practise slash and burn methods to carve out farms from the remaining forests. Mining companies, large farming concerns

and ranchers are also responsible for habitat loss in South America and Asia. In many areas where vast rainforests once proliferated, only desert-like conditions exist today.

The loss of rainforest in South America is critical to the spectacled bear population, while in Asia the sun bear, the sloth bear, the Asian black bear and the giant panda are all affected by diminishing home territories. Giant pandas, one of the most endangered bears, are well-publicized victims of habitat loss. They used to range throughout central and southeast China all the way to Vietnam, but today they are fragmented into 20 small reserves, and it is feared that they may soon become extinct. China, in an effort to avoid this catastrophe, recently opened the vast Caopo Nature Reserve, adjacent to the Wolong Nature Reserve. It is hoped that with this larger reserve, and with Wolong's successful breeding facility, pandas will move back from the brink.

Because of its popularity, the giant panda's plight receives extensive coverage from the press. This helps to obscure the fact that pandas may actually be less endangered today than the small sun bear and the sloth bear. According to scientists, the sun bear is now very difficult to find in the wild and appears to have disappeared completely from many of its old haunts. Malaysia's rainforests provide primary habitat for the sun bear, and the country is being deforested at a rapid rate. The sloth bear has also disappeared from many of its old territories. In the unrelenting competition for land between bears and indigenous human populations, the latter always win.

Habitat loss is not just a tragedy for tropical bears and pandas, but for the grizzly (brown) bear in North America. Hunting, trapping, poaching, road construction, poisoning, and the conversion of bear habitats to farmland and ranches have forced grizzly bears to take refuge in small pockets of remaining wilderness in the northern Rockies, primarily in

A Finnish bear, in what wilderness yet remains.

Yellowstone and Glacier National Parks. Between 800 and 1,000 grizzlies exist in the United States, excluding Alaska. They, too, are now fragmented and separated from a larger Canadian population. A recent effort to open a corridor from Canada's Yukon territory to Yellowstone to encourage freer movement of grizzlies into parts of their old home ranges in Idaho, Wyoming and Montana, was blocked by the George W. Bush administration after appeals from local ranchers and farmers who feared bears would endanger their cattle and sheep. Environmentalists, however, see this corridor as vital to expanding the genetic diversity of the isolated bear populations in this area of the United States.[1] Unfortunately, bears do not have votes. Even in Canada, with the largest brown bear population in North America, some scientists estimate that 60 per cent are now at risk.

Bears' low reproductive rate is another factor posing a problem for maintaining grizzly populations. In Alaska, where there are estimated to be anywhere from 12,000 to 13,000 grizzlies – the highest number in the United States – the interval between litters of cubs is three to five years. Biologists interested in bear preservation note that this interval, combined with small litter sizes of one to two cubs, is a critical factor in their attempts to maintain viable populations, especially in the Greater Yellowstone region. In Yellowstone, where the grizzly population is about 200, of which it is estimated only about 40 are breeding females or sows, 'scientists have calculated that the annual loss of only one or two mature females capable of reproduction may mean the difference between maintaining a stable population and eventual extirpation.'[2] There is even fear for the future of Alaska's grizzlies. Since World War II, the number of humans in Alaska has catapulted from 70,000 to 500,000 and keeps on growing. Human population centres with their widespread garbage dumps act like magnets for bears. Bears that are not shot for venturing too close to residential areas are often poisoned by eating cans, car batteries, engine oil and other toxic substances.[3]

The Arctic is another area where habitat loss poses a serious problem for bears. According to scientists, oil drilling on Alaska's north coast disturbs the denning areas of female polar bears. The bears, extremely sensitive to the noise of drilling, often abort their cubs. Since the polar bear population also grows slowly, scientists fear increased drilling will have a disastrous effect on the region's population. Another problem also threatens the bears. A warming of the Arctic caused by climate change (global warming), is melting ice shelves that polar bears use to hunt seals, their primary food source. Because the ice is melting earlier each spring and reforming later each fall, it is forcing bears to come ashore much earlier and depart later. Whereas summer is the time that bears south of the Arctic feed heavily in preparation for winter hibernation, for polar bears it is a period of near fasting. Bears now have to start their fasts earlier and continue them much longer. Hence, polar bears are weaker than in the past by the time winter sets in and they can start their winter hunts. This is critical for pregnant bears since they may not have accumulated enough fat to survive the cub-bearing season. Cubs born under such conditions have less chance of survival since their mothers produce less milk and what milk there is, is less nourishing.[4]

Poaching is still another major problem. The polar bear population is presently listed as being between 22,000 and 27,000. Many of them live in the Siberian Arctic. The closure of military bases and Arctic research stations has led to a rise in poverty in the region and a major increase in bear poaching. Poaching estimates range from less than 100 to as many as 1,000 per annum, but even at the lower figure it will be hard to sustain the Siberian polar bear population.

A polar bear
being captured
in Greenland.

Toxic wastes are also threatening polar bears. Although
these bears dine almost exclusively on seals, they seldom eat the
whole animal, preferring to eat only the skin and the layers of
blubber beneath. But toxic wastes accumulate in these fat tissues, so through eating the blubber, they become walking toxic
waste dumps. Scientists have recently found hermaphrodite
polar bears – bears with the organs of both sexes – in the waters
above Norway, which they attribute to an accumulation of poly-

chlorinated biphenyls (PCBS) or other chemicals that disrupt normal hormone functioning in the tissues. Here, in a part of the ocean that is far from industrial sources of pollution, the residue of such chemicals as PCBS and DDT is a potent 90 parts per million in bears, and scientists believe this is to be a primary cause of the bears' low birth rate.[5] For some time it was suspected that the deformities were caused by PCBS and other industrial pollutants that mimic the hormone oestrogen, but there was no firm proof.[6] But the Arctic Monitoring and Assessment Program, based in Norway, has confirmed that polar bears, along with seals and other arctic mammals, are showing significant contamination from several industrial toxins including PCBS and mercury. These chemicals are carried by fish and other marine life as well as by winds and ocean currents. More research is needed on what effects these toxic chemicals will have on bear reproduction.[7]

Foreign species or exotics introduced into their natural habitats, along with pollution, are also serious problems for maintaining healthy bear populations. In North America grizzly bears are now pretty well confined to Alaska and the northern Rocky Mountains in the United States, to the mountains of western Canada, and to Mexico. In the fall many grizzlies move to higher elevations to feast on meaty pine nuts produced in great abundance by the whitebark pine. Unfortunately, this pine species is being killed off by a fungus from Eurasia called blister rust. Beginning in 1905, this fungal disease became endemic in the eastern white pine forests of North America when it was introduced by seedlings brought over from Europe. In time, blister rust spread both westward and upward to the high elevation forests of whitebark pines. This is depriving grizzlies of a major dietary supplement.[8] According to Kerry Gunther, a bear management specialist in Yellowstone National Park, with the demise of the whitebark pine, birth rates for grizzlies are likely to fall and death rates to rise.[9] An added problem is the loss of the 'refuge effect', that is, the loss of pine nuts means that bears will no longer be drawn to higher altitudes away from the dangers of close proximity to human populations, especially hunters during hunting season.

Grizzly bears in the northern Rockies have five main sources of food: animals, mainly winter kill; whitebark pine nuts and other vegetation; spawning cutthroat trout and army cutworm moths. Cutthroat trout have also been increasingly in danger because non-native lake trout are illegally introduced into Yellowstone's lakes by sport fishermen. Lake trout are fierce predators and ichthyologists predict that the cutthroat trout population could be cut by 70 per cent in the near future.[10]

Another concern is the effect of brucellosis on the Yellowstone bear population. The spread of this disease among the Park's bison and elk populations worries surrounding cattle ranchers, who are fearful that the disease may spread to their cattle, so plans are being discussed to cull at least some of the elk. This would further reduce bears' nutrients since these ungulates – especially the calves – constitute an important part of their diet. This could induce Yellowstone bears to forage outside the park boundaries in search of food, putting them at greater risk with local human populations.

But it is the army cutworm moths that present perhaps the greatest problem. Grizzlies feed heavily on these moths for three to four months of the year. It is estimated that one bear can eat from 20,000 to 40,000 moths a day and, because they are a rich source of nutrients, obtain as many as 30,000 calories a day! Unfortunately, changing land use in the Great Plains together with climate change may have an adverse affect on army cutworm moth populations. The moths ingest large quantities of pesticides and since bears eat the moths in such great numbers, the pesticides or toxins accumulate in the bears' tissues at a rapid rate, as with polar bears eating seal blubber, causing sickness, genetic abnormalities and even death.[11]

Preserving and protecting the grizzly bear population in Yellowstone is difficult and complex. This can be seen in the evolution of management policy. In the early years of the park, to entertain the guests, bears were fed every evening. As early as 1891, park officials complained that bears were becoming a nuisance as they searched around the lodges for garbage. By 1910, bears standing alongside park roads were panhandling food from tourists. In 1916 Yellowstone recorded the first human death from a bear attack. Between 1931 and 1969, Yellowstone bears inflicted an average of 48 injuries on humans each year. Partly in an effort to counteract this problem, park officials devised a bear management programme in 1970. One of the restrictions called for the immediate removal of all garbage dumps. This ignited a long-simmering dispute between the park manager and noted biologists, John and Frank Craighead. The Craigheads, two of the world's leading specialists on grizzlies, urged a gradual removal of the dumps. They predicted that without the dumps, bear–human conflicts would increase both in the park and beyond its borders, resulting in the deaths of many grizzlies.

Just as they feared, in the first two years following the closure of the dumps, 88 grizzlies were killed in or near the park, more than in Yellowstone's entire history. So many were killed that by 1975 grizzlies in the Greater Yellowstone ecosystem were listed as a threatened species. This initiated the Bear Recovery Plan, which many believed would be expensive to run and difficult to assess. They were right. In 1983 the Inter-Agency Grizzly Bear Committee was established to coordinate efforts to rescue the region's bear population. Although the bears today show some signs of recovering from the massive slaughter of the 1970s, it is too early to tell if present policies will achieve complete success. Hampered by a lack of genetic diversity and prevented by surrounding human encroachment from ranging freely and mixing with Canadian bears, the Yellowstone area's grizzly population remains weak and threatened.

Similar ecological problems are impacting bears in other areas of the world. The worldwide spread of industrial pollutants into rivers and oceans, especially PCBs and mercury, has resulted in dangerously high concentrations in salmon, seals and many other maritime creatures. Coastal brown bears that rely heavily on spawning salmon and who – like polar bears – often ignore the meat, eating primarily the skin, fat and roe, end up ingesting the very tissues in which these chemicals are stored.

A recent study on the Asian trade in bears and bear parts carried out by Judy Mills and Christopher Servheen under the auspices of the WWF, asserts that the trade in bear parts is a threat to bears' survival equal to or greater than the loss of habitat.[12] The most sought after parts are gall bladders. These form part of traditional Chinese medicine and, gram for gram, fetch as much on the black market as heroin. In 1991 they fetched eighteen times the price of equivalent weights of gold. Other bear parts are also extremely profitable. In the same year, 1991, it was estimated that the market value of an adult bear, including its gall bladder, paws, hide, claws, bones and meat, was about $10,000.

It is difficult to estimate the number of bears killed in Asia for their body parts, but if the numbers of gall bladders are any indication, it must be in the thousands. In the markets of many cities in China and southeast Asia, dried gall bladders are displayed for sale in stall after stall. Even in Singapore, where there

Spinal cord good for deafness, giddiness, promotes hair growth and prevents dandruff.

Grease from bear's back invigorates mind, prevents hunger, promotes longevity. It also prevents numbness, is a cold remedy, blacken hair, prevents baldness, ringworm and prevents pimples.

Head popular as Decorative item.

Hides used for wall hangings.

Blood prevents nervousness in children.

Bear body-parts used for traditional medicine.

Meat good for rheumatism and beri-beri.

Gallbladder good for heart disease, digestive systems and liver disease. Also used for blindness in infants, hemorrhoids, conjunctivitis, infant colic and tooth decay.

Bones prevents rheumatism and nervousness in children.

Paw prevents colds renews energy. Also bear-paw soup is a popular and expensive dish in much of Asia.

Claws serve as good luck charms in some Asian countries.

is a law against selling bear parts, they can easily be found in the marketplace. Of course, not all the gall bladders come from Asian bears. An international smuggling trade in bear parts includes Canada, the United States, eastern Europe and South America. Nor does the number of bears killed for their body parts reflect the extent of the trade and the actual drop in bear numbers in the wilderness. Many adult bears are killed in order to capture cubs, which are then sold in Asia as pets or to bear 'farms', where tubes are inserted into their gall bladders, generally without the use of anaesthetics and they are, in an agonizing process, constantly 'milked' of their bile.

A selection of
products at a
bear-bile farm
in China, 2000.

A bear-bile farm in China, 2000.

In 1991, there were 30 major bear farms in China holding more than 100 bears, as well as many smaller farms. Currently China plans farms capable of holding 40,000 bile-producing bears. Bear farms in North Korea, where the practice began, have been operating for over 30 years. Several other Asian nations are eager to start up farms of their own. Because of the growing scarcity of bears in the wild, especially black bears that are reputed to give the highest quality bile, Chinese officials see the milking of bears as a 'conservation' measure; a better solution than killing wild bears for their gall bladders. It would be of little comfort to the bears that spend much of their lives in

A cage close up at a bear-bile farm.

pain, enduring pus-filled abscesses and confined in cages too small to turn around in, to know that they are suffering for the sake of their wild brethren. Though 'bear bile' can now be produced artificially in laboratories and is sold in pill form, many Asians reject both the pills and the 'milked bile', claiming these are less efficacious than the bile of wild bears.[13]

The 'conservation' rationale for bear farms is not nearly as meritorious as Chinese officials want people to believe. The farms pose a setback for bear conservation efforts in China. Instead of conservationists working to learn more about bear ecology in order to protect bears and their habitats, they are devoting their efforts to developing more effective breeding programmes for captive bears and seeking ways to increase bile production. Very little is known about Asian bear ecology, and without such knowledge it becomes even harder to assure the survival of wild bears.

Bear farms are also an excellent way to move illegally acquired bears and bear parts into the market. Under the Convention on International Trade in Endangered Species or Wild Fauna and Flora (CITES), there are many loopholes that facilitate the bear trade. Since it is difficult to distinguish between parts from captive-bred bears or bear parts and those acquired in the wild, the illegal trade flourishes. It is easy to produce false documentation, and because minimal records are kept anyway, it is a simple matter to circumvent the system. In turn, the ease with which bears and their parts are moved in and out of bear farms encourages poaching and illegal trading.

The same is true of bear parks in Japan where, according to Mills and Servheen, a secret international trade in bear parts flourishes. As of 1991, there were eight bear parks in Japan with one more under construction and another proposed. Altogether, they house around 1,000 bears, including all bear species except pandas. In most the bears' living conditions are deplorable. They live out miserable lives crowded together and surrounded by concrete. In one park, adult bears averaged only 1,551 square ft (13 m²) of space during the day and 614 square ft (1.3 m²) at night. They are fed on restaurant scraps and have been known to die after swallowing sticks used to skewer chickens for cooking. There is a good deal of fighting among the males, and many die with their wounds left unattended while others just drop dead. The most aggressive bears are placed in isolation and starved until they lose the energy to fight.[14]

These parks also promote the selling of bear parts to tourists. According to Mills and Servheen, one park sold bear meat in small souvenir cans and bear skins with the paws and head attached. In one park in 1991, canned meat sales brought in about $3,000 while bear rugs fetched $3,000 each. One bear park allows preferred Korean and Japanese customers to select a bear from which the gall bladder is to be taken. The chosen animal is then isolated and starved because it is believed that starving makes the gall bladder grow larger. When the bear is 'ready', an air-driven hammer is used to stun it, and killing is completed by cutting its throat.[15]

Tourists enjoy the bear parks for the entertainment they provide. They can watch bears participating in circus-like acts or fighting over food scraps. Some parks provide visitors with plastic guns that shoot food. A few have small learning centres that provide information on bears worldwide. Nonetheless, critics of bear parks see them as 'agents' that launder bear gall bladders and other parts for profit, stimulating the commercial trade in bears while failing to promote the conservation of wild bears.

Mills and Servheen believe the trade in bears and bear parts will escalate, and as bears disappear from Asia, those elsewhere will supply the trade.[16] To some extent, this is already happening.

Evidence from Canada and the United States includes bears found dead in national parks with their gall bladders and paws removed. The increasing levels of affluence in Asia, the opening of borders and escalating trade worldwide, paint a grim picture for the future of bears, especially when the profits to be made are so high (some Chinese and Korean bear parts poachers in Siberia, for example, dissemble as timber industry workers).

It will be hard to bring an end to this trade. Part of the problem is the difficulty in enforcing international regulations against trade in endangered species set forth under CITES. Those who attempt to do so are often powerless to prevent illegal trafficking in bear parts or the selling of bears to farms, parks or private individuals as pets because of the way bears are classified. CITES places them in three main categories under Appendices I to III, with Appendix I listing the most critically endangered species. This first group includes sun bears, Asiatic black bears, giant pandas, Tibetan brown bears, Himalayan brown bears and Mexican grizzlies. These bears are considered to be the most threatened by extinction and are therefore – supposedly – protected. Appendix II lists American and European brown bears (outside Russia), and polar bears. These bears, while not presently considered threatened with extinction, certainly may be in the near future if strict regulation against their trade is not enforced. Appendix III lists only the Canadian black bear. This third level enables countries to call on others for aid in helping to protect a species from extinction. Obviously, not all bears receive equal protection.

Added to what many consider to be major defects in the present CITES rankings for bear protection is the fact that not all countries are signatories. Although some Asian countries are party to CITES, many of their neighbours are not, facilitating the illegal smuggling and sale of bears. As of 1991, Bhutan,

Myanmar (Burma), Cambodia, South Korea, Laos, Taiwan and Vietnam had not joined CITES. This means that bear traffickers who acquire bears or bear parts in a country that has joined CITES need only say that they acquired them in a non-CITES country to gain permission to sell the bears or their parts back in the CITES country. For example, bears illegally killed by poachers in Thailand can be smuggled into Cambodia and then brought back 'legally' into Thailand simply by claiming they were acquired in Cambodia. Under such conditions, and because it is so difficult to determine either the true provenance of bears or bear parts or their legal status, customs officials increasingly do not even try.

Some Asian countries have imposed their own regulations regarding the sale or exploitation of bears, but again it is easy to circumvent these laws simply by claiming that the bear or bear parts came from somewhere else. In Singapore, conservation officials point out that to prove a crime not only must the dealers in bear parts be caught in the act, but that even when people are caught, all they have to do is argue that the parts came from American black bears or Russian brown bears or were acquired before Singapore signed up to CITES. Since no documentation is required, it is difficult to prove otherwise. Some conservation officers point out that it is hard to distinguish bear gall bladders from pig gall bladders, making positive identification even more difficult. Even in the United States, laws vary among states regarding the sale of bear parts. The same applies to Canada and its provinces.[17]

Yet another problem in the enforcement of CITES is the frustratingly complex procedure necessary to make an arrest. Poachers who flaunt regulations and use loopholes are nearly impossible to stop. That being so, why is the trade not curtailed at the market end by arresting those who sell to the public?

Wildlife dealers in Singapore say that government agents will never learn enough about the illicit trade to achieve anything effective 'because everyone involved knows everyone else, and a law enforcement officer would be obvious to them'.[18] Those who carry out the trade are well versed in the law and know how to get round the restrictions. In Cambodia, even though it is not a party to the CITES convention, there are laws regulating the trade in bears and bear parts but there are so many loopholes that it is easy to evade prosecution.

In *Search for the Golden Moon Bear*, Sy Montgomery illustrates the problem of enforcement. When she and an officer from the Wildlife Protection Office visited a stall in Cambodia filled with illegal bear parts, the woman who owned the stall smiled and nodded to the officer knowing he could not do anything. As the officer explained, the stall also served as her residence, bringing it under a different set of regulations. To search a residence, the officer claimed he had to obtain signatures from several other agencies and then collect a force of about ten agents. This would give plenty of warning, so that by the time the agents arrived to confiscate the illegal bear parts they would have 'disappeared'. According to Montgomery's source, some dealers would not hesitate to murder anyone who tries to interfere.

Interpol considers the trade in wildlife the second largest illegal trade in the world (second only to the drugs trade), and those who deal in wildlife also often deal in drugs, arms and people (including the slave trade and prostitution). The agents trying to stop the trade claim that poachers and traffickers in wildlife are as organized as the Mafia and pose as much danger. It is little wonder that agents often think twice before trying to enforce laws against poachers and sellers of bears and bear parts and that protecting bears under CITES is so difficult.[19] Mills and Servheen report that when a Thai conservation officer caught wildlife traffickers poaching bear, she was warned 'her health would be in danger if she did not back down'. They noted 'corruption was widespread and well known'.[20]

In India and China, bear meat is used in traditional medicine, but in much of southeast Asia, China and Japan it is also served in culinary delicacies, including bear-paw soup. It even appeared on the menu at a prestigious Western hotel chain's restaurant in Seoul, South Korea. Bear paws first became popular as a delicacy during the Ming Dynasty (1368–1644) in China. They are even mentioned by Topsell as being considered a tasty dish in England in the early seventeenth century.[21] The appreciation of the dish spread through most of southeast Asia, and the cost of this culinary delight has contributed to the decimation of bear populations. Just one shipment of bear paws weighing 8,800 lb (4,000 kg) intercepted in 1990 in a Chinese port represented 1,000 bears killed by forestry officials working with Chinese and Japanese merchants. In Japan, it is legal to kill 'nuisance' bears. Since farmers can greatly supplement their incomes by selling them, any bear seen becomes a 'nuisance', often ending up on a plate in an upper-class restaurant.[22]

Although bear paw soup can be found on the menus of many Chinese restaurants throughout Asia, it miraculously vanishes when conservation officers come through the door. The dish is extremely expensive, and to ensure that it is fresh, or that the patron receives the left front paw – considered by tradition to be the tastiest because many believe it is the paw bears use to gather honey – orders have to be placed several days in advance. Some restaurants keep live bears on the premises to assure the paws' freshness. As orders are received, the bears' paws are cut off, starting with the front left, until the tortured animals are left to hobble around on four bloody stumps. To curtail their anguished cries, their vocal cords are cut. It is almost impossible to comprehend their suffering.[23] But laws against such cruelty and the sale of bear body parts are hard to enforce when the majority of the population resists their enforcement. Thus the profits remain great while the risks of fining or imprisonment are small.

According to at least one report, people from several countries of southeast Asia visit Thailand on bear-eating tours. Although Thais refrain from eating bear meat, several restaurants owned by Koreans or Chinese serve it. Despite Thailand being a signatory of CITES, bears are frequently hunted for the trade. Mills and Servheen interviewed one person 'who witnessed a hunter carrying a poached bear back to a camp inside Thailand's Khao Yai National Park, where nearly 60 poacher camps existed at that time'.[24] Traders in wildlife often enlist poor villagers living on the edges of national parks in Thailand to poach bears and other animals. If a dealer obtains an order for a particular animal, all he needs to do is alert these villagers, expediting the order and avoiding the delays that hunting for the animal on the black market would incur. 'Entire villages on the fringes of national parks [in Thailand] survive on the poaching trade that feeds the wildlife restaurants of Asia.'[25] In Taiwan, a similar situation exists. Mills and Servheen claim that three bears were killed for their gall bladders in the Lala Mountain Reserve, a sanctuary set up to protect them. The hunters claim that by ignoring the Wildlife Conservation Law in Taiwan, they can make about $2,700 for each bear killed.[26] The dealers who purchase these bears make even more on their resale.

In 1991, a raid by the Thai Crime Suppression Division on a farm south of Bangkok found 4 freshly killed bears and some 40 people, mostly Koreans, feasting on the meat. They also found several live bears, more hidden in a nearby village, a refrigerator filled with 48 bear paws, and records of the sale of bear gall bladders and paws. The farm was advertised in Korea and Taiwan as a restaurant and outlet for traditional medicine. 'Sixteen tour companies had been bringing in groups of tourists from South Korea, Taiwan and Hong Kong to eat protected [bear] species and buy medicine made from their parts.' Several Chinese medicine shops were associated with the farm, which also provided bear meat for Korean restaurants in Bangkok. The bears were smuggled to the farm by boat from Cambodia and overland from Myanmar (Burma) and hidden in the surrounding region. The farm itself was kept under tight security and bears were killed only on order. 'The farm's owner, brother of Thailand's deputy commerce minister, claimed the farm was a zoo set up for tourists and to help save endangered animals from extinction.'[27]

Several approaches have been suggested to try and counter the decline in bear populations worldwide. One suggestion is that bear eggs and sperm be frozen in a process known as cryogenics, and kept in freezers until conditions in the wild are more advantageous for bear survival. While this is probably possible, who will teach the cubs how to survive in their new environments? Mother bears do far more than just give birth to cubs. They 'acculturate' them to their surroundings over a period of about two years, teaching them to hunt and where and when to find plants and other food sources, in short, how to interact with and survive in their particular ecosystems.

Less radical suggestions include building special bear reserves or preserving them in zoos. Reserves can be effective in species' preservation but they have their limits. Small reserves are more acceptable to surrounding human populations, but this demands the constant culling of the animals to keep their numbers down to a level their food supplies can healthily maintain. Larger reserves are superior but are less easy to defend against growing human populations that constantly cross the reserve's borders seeking fuel, meat and cropland. Sometimes large reserves are built across the territories of two distinct bear subspecies, resulting in the extinction of both. Many feel that several reserves in a particular area should be connected to each other by corridors. Others think that corridors could help to spread disease, and ask whether bears would actually use them.

Zoological parks or gardens are valuable in the short term. Most of the larger zoos worldwide are careful not to allow inter-breeding and scrupulously comply with stud book regulations. But the rising costs involved in keeping each animal poses a constant challenge to zoos, a challenge they are sometimes unable to meet. Besides the financial costs involved, zoos also find bears very difficult to keep, since these strong, intelligent and observant animals all too often manage to effect escapes, creating panic. Bears, especially polar bears, are prone to stereo-typing, a term used to denote repetitive behaviour like pacing and head swinging, which incurs public criticisms of zoos. Although there are several levels of stereotyping, some of which are natural, the general public is not aware of this and zoos are often accused of maltreatment.

Some zoos have tried to capitalize on their conservation func-tion by reporting their progress in introducing captive bred animals back into the wild. Reintroduction programmes, though, are not only very expensive to plan and carry out, but do not always work. It is easier to reintroduce herding animals to their former habitats than solitary animals like bears. Another problem in introducing bears back into the wild is that there is increasingly less wild left.[28] In 2002, Seattle's Woodland Park Zoo celebrated the birth of a sloth bear, an endangered species. The zoo participates in the Species Survival Plan and notes that although there are only 48 sloth bears in captivity their goal is eventually to have more than 60. They hope to be able to introduce the zoo-bred animals back into the wild. Unfortunately, as the zoo points out, the bears' natural habitats in southeast Asia are rapidly disappearing while poachers eagerly await new arrivals. So will zoos' bear reintroduction programmes merely serve to enrich poachers?

In many parts of South America, economic conditions closely resemble those existing in parts of Asia. Poor farmers barely eke out a subsistence living. Killing spectacled bears often gives them the means to survive. Besides its meat and skin, the bears furnish fat, organs, blood and bones. The fat is believed to provide relief from rheumatism, blindness, gall bladder attacks and muscular pain. The bones are ground up and given to children in the belief that they will ensure good health. Warm blood is drunk as a general tonic, while eating gall bladders is believed to prevent blindness and cataracts. Some gall bladders find their way to Asia, providing desperately needed cash for peasant farmers.[29]

In some places in South America, the spectacled bear is revered, in others reviled. Myths and legends tell of bears stealing young unmarried women and young boys. Where these stories prevail, bears are killed on sight. But there are other reasons for the spectacled bear's decline. Bears are seen, with some truth, as cattle and sheep killers. Deforestation of much of the bears' territory have driven many of them to seek refuge higher in the mountains, with fewer food resources, and may put their survival at risk. In some areas deforestation has fragmented bear territory, resulting in isolated populations of spectacled bears. Because they live much of their lives in trees and nest in trees at night, deforestation deprives them of a vital environment. This is also true for some bears of southeast Asia. Deforestation forces them to search for new forest areas, which may soon no longer exist.[30]

A 1936 poster for Brookfield Zoo in Illinois – a fanciful view of the bear.

Spectacled bears' habitats are also areas of political unrest, drug production and rebel warfare. Government-ordered aerial spraying of coca plantations as part of the war on drugs kills both vegetation and bears. Spectacled bears are also killed to provide food for rebel armies living in the rainforest.[31]

Bears are often captured and used for display at roadside hotels and restaurants to attract tourists or to be sold as pets. Whether tourist attraction or pet, the bears suffer. Their nutrition is poor; they live in crowded, squalid cages; are prone to disease and abuse and live out their lives in discomfort and pain. Bears kept under such conditions have been known to attack and sometimes kill children. This stirs up antipathy towards bears and encourages the hunting and killing of bears in those areas.[32]

Bear hunting has often been cited as a cause of bear depopulation. As we have seen, it certainly can be in Asia, South America, the Arctic, and in parts of North America, but it does not have to have this effect. Because hunting black bears is a major sport in West Virginia, a mountainous state in the eastern United States, the declining bear population became a cause for concern not only among conservationists but also among hunters. In seeking a solution, the state did not ban hunting but moved the hunting season one month later in the fall. Bear researchers noted that pregnant female bears and females with cubs were the first to begin hibernation in the fall. The second to go into dens were young males and the last the older males. By moving the hunting season females and young male bears were protected from hunters who then only had access to the older males. This led to a marked rise in the bear population. This remedy may be applied in other states where bear hunting is also a fall sport and bear populations have fallen.

Some problems associated with climate change have already been mentioned, but there are other, less apparent yet no less potentially injurious, effects of global warming on bears. As oceans warm, fish like salmon that require colder waters could migrate northward, depriving bears living along the coasts of Washington state and British Columbia of a major source of nutrition. With the one degree of warming experienced so far, bird and animal species are already moving and some plant and tree varieties are also being found further northwards or further up into the mountains. Might whitebark pines, whose pine nuts form a significant part of grizzly bears' diets, move yet higher up mountain slopes until they run out of mountain? In many parts of the world, such northward migration of plants and animals is impossible because of the physical barriers imposed by humans and their infrastructures. Animals are perhaps less affected in this migration process since they can move faster than plants. Even so, they are restricted by fences, highways, dams, urban expansion, new housing developments, and slash and burn agriculture and logging.

Will the plants that bears depend on disappear? Will the spread of plant or insect-borne diseases caused by global warming affect bear populations? Will rising oceans created by ice melting in the Arctic and Antarctic regions flood coastal areas in southeast Asia where sun bears search nightly for insects?

While it is true that bears have survived other major periods of climate change and that they are more adaptable (because of their omnivorous feeding habits) than many other animals, bears have never had to start from such a weakened base and in a world of such enormous habitat loss, toxic waste and increasing human population. There is also evidence that in the past climate changes occurred far more gradually than is happening today. With most bear populations plummeting and many hanging on in isolated communities, survival under climate change conditions is problematical. Just as the cave bear became extinct, so might history repeat itself with one or more of the current bear species.

We do not know how quickly global warming will occur or what its full effects may be on bears; nor do we know whether certain bear populations will be more affected than others. Unfortunately, we probably will not know until it is too late. What we do know is that it is unlikely the present trend of global warming will stop: indeed, scientific computer projections inform us that it will continue through this century and beyond, but will the pace, although fast when compared to earlier periods of warming, be gradual enough for species to have time to adjust and survive? These are important questions for which we have no answers.

Christopher Servheen, who has studied bears all over the world, believes that bear protection efforts should be linked to other conservation programmes. He offers suggestions as to how this might be accomplished. Watershed protection to assure local water supplies could be linked with the protection of forests and sustainable forestry. The practice of sustainable forestry would provide economic incentives to local populations through lumbering and at the same time could stop the fragmentation of bear habitats and assure long-term survival for bear populations. Such programmes would help save bears but would also create jobs and raise standards of living for local populations.[33]

Of course, money is important to put such programmes into effect but it is also needed to educate local populations. Likewise, money is essential for research, dissemination of research findings, and for the enforcement of regulations. But regulations are useless without sufficient enforcement and fines high enough to inhibit poaching. It appears that neither local nor national governments in many places can do it all. Enforceable multinational agreements are required and international organizations like the United Nations, the WWF, TRAFFIC, and the World Society for the Protection of Animals are all vital to provide the required education and support for conservation.

The international CITES agreement of 1973 signalled a major attempt to control the trade in endangered species. While flaws in this agreement exist where bears are concerned, the flaws may be less in the agreement itself than in its enforcement and in the fact that several countries have so far chosen not to sign up. Other international agreements, although more limited in scope, have proved effective. Beginning in 1965, five countries with polar bear populations – Canada, the Soviet Union, Denmark, Norway and the United States – met in Fairbanks,

Alaska, to discuss the protection of polar bears and to work out what steps were needed to be taken to study the bears and their habitats in order to construct a viable conservation plan. Scientists from all five countries developed a plan, the International Agreement on the Conservation of Polar Bears and their Habitat, which was signed at a conference in Oslo, Norway, in 1973. This requires each signatory nation to protect polar bears and their habitats.

> Each Contracting Party shall take appropriate action to protect the ecosystems of which polar bears are a part with special attention to habitat components such as denning and feeding sites and migration patterns and shall manage polar bear populations in accordance with sound conservation practices based on the best scientific data.[34]

Although the agreement has no enforcement mechanism, the polar bear population has rebounded since the 1960s. The George W. Bush administration's attempts to turn the Alaskan National Wildlife Refuge (ANWR), a prime denning ground for polar bears, into an oil exploration area is now threatening the spirit of this agreement.

Another agreement modelled on the one above is the Inuvialuit–Inupiat Management Agreement on Polar Bears in the southern Beaufort Sea. The Inuvialuit of Canada and the Inupiat of Alaska hunt the same polar bear population. The Inuvialuit hunt, however, is confined to certain seasons and the kills are recorded. The Inupiat hunt was not regulated, neither as to season nor to the number of animals killed. For example, there were no restrictions on killing cubs, females with cubs, or bears in dens. This placed a strain on the bear population in the border area between the two groups. To effect a solution, the

Inuvialuit and Inupiat came together and worked out an agreement setting out regulations to create a sustainable bear population in the disputed area. Although it is still too early to see how effective the agreement will be, it is important because it is an example of two peoples coming together and, without outside help, agreeing to control hunts and the numbers and sexes of bears killed. It is hoped that such agreements might be reached in other parts of the world among indigenous peoples.[35]

An important international programme working for the protection of Arctic wildlife including the polar bear is the Arctic Monitoring and Assessment Program headquartered in Norway. There are also national government programmes. The Canadian Wildlife Service and the us Fish and Wildlife Service with its Marine Mammal Management Program in Alaska are both concerned with the conservation of polar bears.

Several organizations and non-governmental organizations (NGOs), have stepped in to help. The International Bear Biology Association (IBBA) has promoted research on bears. Begun in 1966 with a small group of biologists meeting in Whitehorse, Yukon Territory, Canada, IBBA now holds conferences every three years to ever larger groups of researchers. Other organizations, such as the Grizzly Bear Education and Conservation Campaign, Black Bear Awareness, Inc., the Greater Yellowstone Coalition, the Yellowstone Grizzly Foundation, Grizzly Discovery Center, the Black Bear Institute and the North American Bear Center, include in their mission statements a focus on educating the public about bears.

Larger organizations, some of them with international programmes, not only support conservation and habitat protection but also promote research and education. Such organizations are not totally preoccupied with bears and their survival, but many grant support to programmes that benefit bear research and conservation. These larger organizations include the WWF, TRAFFIC, USA, Defenders of Wildlife, The Wilderness Society, World Society for the Protection of Animals (WSPA), the National Wildlife Federation (NWF), the International Fund for Animal Welfare (IFAW), Wildlife Conservation International, and the International Union for the Conservation of Nature and Natural Resources (IUCN). The last named has set up species survival commissions on various endangered animals. It maintains separate commissions for individual bear species, such as the polar bear, spectacled bear and others.

Survival for several bear species is possible because bears are intelligent animals and masters at adapting to unfamiliar surroundings, but they must be given the chance to adapt. If some biologists are correct in proclaiming that in the future no wildernesses will exist, artificial ones must be created or preserved from the remains of those still existing. This will take not only money but education, dedication and sound management. Bears are known as a 'flagship' species: that is, if bears disappear they will take other species, both plant and animal, with them. The biodiversity of their former habitats will suffer. The creation of reserves that provide open corridors to other reserves is not enough. Reserves must be carefully managed and guarded against poachers, disease and over-crowding. There must be reserves not just for bears but for the entire megafauna necessary for bear survival. Several reserves are currently in various stages of completion but will they be large enough and will they be ready soon enough? Will the stamina and political will be there in the future to assure their continuance and pay for their sound management? As American ecologist Aldo Leopold pointed out in the early decades of the twentieth century, once man starts managing nature, he can never stop.

I prefer to close on a story of hope. One recent bear reserve started in an unusual way. It began with the British Broadcasting Company (BBC) making a documentary on the origins of Paddington Bear. According to the story by Michael Bond, this bear travelled all the way from the dark jungles of Peru, ending up in Paddington Station with a sign around his neck reading 'Please Look After This Bear, Thank You'. Since Paddington's introduction in 1956, he has become famous all over the world. Although the documentary focused on the little stuffed bear from Peru, the show, hosted by actor Stephen Fry, brought the plight of the Peruvian spectacled bear to the attention of the British public. The Paddington Bear documentary was followed by a second documentary, also hosted by Fry, on the creation of a sanctuary for spectacled bears. The bear reserve was the brainchild of Nick Green of OR Media. While

Bear-hunting in Finland today.

167

involved with the Paddington Bear documentary for the BBC, Green grew distressed about the plight of spectacled bears and their declining numbers. In his charming book *Rescuing the Spectacled Bear: A Peruvian Diary*, Fry writes of Green and the bear-saving expedition to deepest, darkest Peru:

> We (and by 'we' I mean primarily Nick, who has led this initiative from first to last and without whose demonic energy and enterprise nothing would ever have been done) decided within a week or so of returning to England [after the first documentary], that another programme should be made devoted this time entirely to the Spectacled Bear and that a charitable foundation should be established for the purpose of rescuing distressed bears, purchasing land for their exclusive use and to pursue research into their numbers, their habitat, behaviour and future.[36]

The result was the Bear Rescue Foundation, which purchased land in Peru and hopes, with public contributions, to purchase even more land in order to create a reserve for spectacled bears. This is a start to counter the decline in this bear's population in South America. The situation is now critical for spectacled bears. Despite the setting aside of Peru's Manu National Park of 5,918 square miles (15,328 km^2), declared an International Biosphere Reserve in 1977, the park and its spectacled bear population are under threat from cattle ranchers, gold miners, oil companies and timber interests that are all seeking access to its resources. These exploitative, short-sighted economic interests bode ill for the bears. But the formation of the Bear Rescue Foundation and of other organizations and foundations provides hope that it is still not too late to turn around the future of spectacled bears and of other bear species around the world. In his article 'The Future of Bears in the Wild', Servheen makes an astute observation while issuing a portentous warning: 'Today, the bears that remain must contend with humans in order to survive, and humans never lose in competition but to themselves.'[37]

Bears and humans have wandered the earth together for millennia. Bears have lumbered around in our memories and our dreams. They have given us comfort and have inhabited our fears. Over time and among many peoples, humans have shared a kinship with bears. If we lose the bear we lose not only an important part of our rich natural heritage but a part of ourselves. Surely it is time to dust off Michael Bond's original request and enlarge on it: 'Please Look After These Bears. Thank You'.

Timeline of the Bear

27 million BC	1.5 million BC	300,000 BC	100,000 BC
Dawn bear roamed parts of Europe. This earliest member of the Ursidae family was about the size of a small terrier and probably looked much like a raccoon	*Ursus etruscus* evolved and became a direct ancestor of the brown bear, American and Asian black bears, sloth bear and the sun bear	*Ursus spelaeus*, the great European cave bear, roamed much of Europe	Encounters between bears and humans led to paintings of bears in the caves of western Europe and perhaps to bear cults

4th century AD	8th century AD	c. 500–800	c. 1000	1580
St Blaise, patron saint of Candlemas, is associated with bears since Candlemas occurs in the spring when bears emerge from their winter dens	Norse warriors who took on the frenzied attributes of bears in battle were known as berserkers and were greatly feared throughout northern Europe	Common for bears to be associated with chieftainships or kingships, as with the legendary King Arthur and Beowulf	An early menagerie at the abbey of St Gall in Switzerland included bears	Charles IX of France includes bears in his animal park in Paris

1872	1894	1902	1911	1926
Yellowstone Park is founded, which will serve as the main refuge for grizzly bears in the United States outside Alaska	Rudyard Kipling publishes *The Jungle Book* and introduces children to the bear Baloo	The first teddy bear is made in Brooklyn, New York, by Morris Michton, followed closely by the Steiff bears made by Margarette Steiff in Gingen-an-der-Brenz, Germany	The British Parliament outlaws dancing bears	*Winnie the Pooh* by A. A. Milne is published, and it quickly becomes a children's classic

40,000 BC	285 BC	c. AD 30	2nd century AD
Cult objects and figurines portraying bears originated about this time	It is recorded that a great white bear at Ptolemy II's court was paraded through the streets of Alexandria on ceremonial occasions	The Roman emperor Caligula killed 400 bears in the Colosseum in one day	Bears are pitted against humans and other animals in the Colosseum in Rome

1607	1804	1835	1837	1869
Edward Topsell includes a description of bears in his bestiary, *History of Four-Footed Beasts*	Meriwether Lewis and William Clark travel across the North American continent and record some of the first accounts of the grizzly bear	The British Parliament makes bear baiting illegal	The children's story *Goldilock's and the Three Bears* is first published in London.	French missionary Père Armand David sends a panda skin to the Paris Museum of Natural History. This is the first record of a panda skin reaching the West

1942	1944	1958	c. 1961	2001
William Faulkner expands his short story 'The Bear' in his collection *Go Down, Moses*	The fire-fighting Smokey Bear first appeared in the United States on posters urging the public to prevent forest fires	Michael Bond creates Paddington Bear, and stories of his adventures are translated into 22 languages	Bear farming to extract bile from bears is begun in North Korea	Berlin's 'Summer of the Bears' entertains tourists and Berliners alike. In the US, the Post Office issues stamps commemorating the teddy bear

References

1 URSIDAE

1 Much of the data on early bears comes from Björn Kurtén,
   The Cave Bear Story: Life and Death of a Vanished Animal (New
   York, 1976).
2 László Kordos, private conversation, June 2002.
3 Kurtén, *The Cave Bear Story*, p. 122.
4 *Ibid*., p. 146.
5 Kordos, private conversation, June 2002.
6 Stephen J. O'Brien, 'The Molecular Evolution of the Bears', in
   Ian Stirling, ed., *Bears* (San Francisco, 1993), p. 26.

2 SURVIVORS

1 Quoted in Jane Harrison and Hope Mirrless, eds, *The Book of the
   Bears* (London, 1926), p. vii.
2 Blaire Van Valkenburgh, 'The Biology of Bears', in Ian Stirling,
   ed., *Bears* (San Francisco, 1993), pp. 50–61.
3 *Ibid*.
4 *Ibid*.
5 Christopher Servheen, 'The Sun Bear', in Ian Stirling, ed., *Bears*,
   p. 124.
6 Terry Domico, *Bears of the World* (New York, 1966), pp. 22–38.
7 Van Valkenburgh, 'The Biology of Bears', p. 55.
8 Servheen, 'The Sun Bear', pp. 125–6.

9 Ramona and Desmond Morris, *Men and Pandas* (New York, 1966), pp. 22–38.

10 Stephen Jay Gould, 'The Panda's Thumb', in Stephen Jay Gould, *The Panda's Thumb* (New York, 1980), pp. 19–26.

11 Wenshi Pan and Zhi Lu, 'The Giant Panda', in Stirling, *Bears*, pp. 140–45.

12 Donald G. Reid, 'The Asiatic Black Bear', in Stirling, *Bears*, p. 118.

13 *Ibid.*, pp. 119–20.

14 John Seidensticker, 'The Sloth Bear', in Stirling, *Bears*, pp. 128–31.

15 *Ibid*.

16 *Ibid*.

17 Andrew E. Derocher, 'The Coloring of Black Bears', in Stirling, *Bears*, pp. 112–13.

18 Michael R. Pelton, 'The American Black Bear', in Stirling, *Bears*, pp. 111, 114–15.

19 Diana Weinhardt, 'The Spectacled Bear', in Stirling, *Bears*, pp. 134–6.

20 *Ibid.*, pp. 136–7.

21 David Rockwell, *Giving Voice to the Bear* (Niwot, CO, 1991), p. 64.

22 Reuben Gold Thwaites, ed., *Original Journals of the Lewis and Clark Expedition, 1804–1806* (New York, 1959), vol. I, p. 322.

23 Andrew E. Derocher, 'Bear Milk', in Stirling, *Bears*, p. 66.

24 Barry Lopez, *Arctic Dreams: Imagination and Desire in a Northern Landscape* (New York, 1966), p. 82.

25 Charles T. Feazel, *White Bear: Encounters with the Master of the Arctic Ice* (New York, 1990), p. 2.

26 *Ibid.*, pp. 2–3.

27 Lopez, *Arctic Dreams*, p. 69.

28 *Ibid.*, pp. 85–6.

3 THE BEAR OF LEGEND

1 Björn Kurtén, *The Cave Bear Story: Life and Death of a Vanished Animal* (New York, 1976), pp. 83–90.

2 *Ibid.*, pp. 91–4.

3 Árpád Ringer, 'Kultuszok és müvészet', in Gyula Gyenis, Attila Hevesi, László Kordos, Zsolt Mester, Árpád Ringer and Violar T. Dobosi, eds, *Emberelödök Nyomában* (Miskolc, 2001), p. 113.

4 Mietje Germonpré, 'Influence of Climate on Sexual Segregation and Cub Mortality in Pleniglacial Cave Bear', in Roel C.G.M. Lauwerier and Ina Plug, eds, *The Future from the Past* (Oxford, 2002), p. 59.

5 A. I. Hallowell, 'Bear Ceremonialism in the Northern Hemisphere', *American Anthropologists*, n.s. (1926), p. 145.

6 Samuli Paulaharju, *Sommpio* (Helsinki, 1939), pp. 196–7.

7 Ella E. Clark, *Indian Legends of the Pacific Northwest* (Berkeley, CA, 1965), pp. 9–11.

8 Elias Lönnrot, ed., *The Kalevala*, trans. Keith Bosley (New York, 1989), p. 607.

9 Lauri Honko, Senni Timonen and Michael Branch, eds, *The Great Bear: A Thematic Anthology of Oral Poetry in Finno-Ugrian Languages*, trans. Keith Bosley (Helsinki, 1993), p. 125.

10 Paul Shepard and Barry Sanders, *The Sacred Paw: the Bear in Nature, Myth and Literature* (New York, 1985), pp. 58–9. For another version, see David Rockwell, *Giving Voice to the Bear* (Niwot, CO, 1991), pp. 116–21.

11 Olaus Magnus, *Description of the Northern Peoples*, ed. Peter Foote, trans. Peter Fisher and Humphrey Higgins (London, 1998), vol. III, pp. 712–13.

12 Charles T. Feazel, *White Bear: Encounters with the Master of the Arctic Ice* (New York, 1990), p. 95.

13 Georgina Loucks, 'The Girl and the Bear Facts: A Cross-Cultural Comparison', *The Canadian Journal of Native Studies*, V (1958), pp. 237–9.

14 Honko, Timonen and Branch, *The Great Bear*, pp. 125–6, 160.

15 Rockwell, *Giving Voice to the Bear*, p. 79.

16 *Ibid.*, p. 77.

17 Alice Marriott and Carol K. Rachlin, eds, *American Indian Mythology* (New York, 1968), pp. 76–9.

18 Shepard and Sanders, *The Sacred Paw*, pp. 113–14.

19 Magnus, *Description of the Northern Peoples*, vol. III, p. 913.

20 Leo Tolstoy, 'The Three Bears', in Jane Harrison and Hope Mirrless, eds, *The Book of the Bear* (London, 1926), pp. 70–74.

21 Honko, Timonen and Branch, *The Great Bear*, p. 120.

4 BEARS AND HUMANS

1   Fred Bruemmer, 'Arctic Treasures', *Natural History* (June 1989), p. 41.

2   J.M.C. Toynbee, *Animals in Roman Life and Art* (Ithaca, NY, 1973), pp. 93–4.

3   *Ibid.*, p. 99.

4   *Ibid.*, p. 17.

5   Lauri Honko, Senni Timonen and Michael Branch, eds, *The Great Bear: A Thematic Anthropology of Oral Poetry in the Finno-Ugrian Languages*, trans. Keith Bosley (Helsinki, 1993), p. 71.

6   *Ibid*

7   *Ibid.*, pp. 125–6.

8   Carl-Martin Edsman, 'The Story of the Bear Wife in Nordic Tradition', *Ethnos*, XXI (1956), pp. 51–2.

9   Paul Shepard and Barry Sanders, *The Sacred Paw: The Bear in Nature, Myth, and Literature* (New York, 1985), p. 122.

10 Alexander Milovsky, 'Hail to Thee, Papa Bear', *Natural History* (December 1993), p. 35.

11 Shepard and Sanders, *The Sacred Paw*, pp. 129, 144.

12 Joyce E. Salisbury, The *Beast Within: Animals in the Middle Ages* (New York, 1994), pp. 3–4.

13 Shepard and Sanders, *The Sacred Paw*, pp. 132–3.

14 *Ibid.*, p. 138.

15 *Ibid.*, p. 132.

16 Nona C. Flores, 'The Mirror of Nature Distorted: the Medieval Artist's Dilemma in Depicting Animals', in Joyce E. Salisbury, ed., *The Medieval World of Nature: A Book of Essays* (New York, 1993), pp. 7–9.

17 Richard Barber, 'Introduction', in *Bestiary: Being an English Version of the Bodleian Library, Oxford M.S. Bodley 764*, trans. Richard Barber (Woodbridge, Suffolk, 1992), pp. 7–9.

18 *Ibid.*, p. 9.

19 *Ibid.*, pp. 58–60.

20 Shepard and Sanders, *The Sacred Paw*, p. 139.

21 Albertus Magnus, *On Animals: A Medieval 'Summa Zoologica'*, trans. Kenneth F. Kitchell, Jr and Irven Michael Resnick (Baltimore, 1991), vol. I, p. 659.

22 Barber, *Bestiary*, pp. 58–60.

23 Olaus Magnus, *Description of the Northern Peoples*, ed. Peter Foote, trans. Peter Fisher and Humphrey Higgins (London, 1998), vol. III, pp. 912–6.

24 Edward Topsell, *The History of Four-Footed Beasts and Serpents and Insects* [1607] (New York, 1967), vol. I, p. 29.

25 *Ibid.*, pp. 30–33.

26 Andre Leroi-Gourham, 'Animals of the Old Stone Age', in A. Houghton Roderick, ed., *Animals in Archaeology* (New York, 1972), p. 6.

27 Barry Sanders, 'The Bear in Literature and Art', in Ian Stirling, ed., *Bears* (San Francisco, 1993), p. 172.

28 Sir William Jardine, ed., 'Introduction to Mammalia', in *The Naturalist's Library* (Edinburgh, 1840), vol. xv, pp. 236–7.

29 Mary Sayre Haverstock, *An American Bestiary* (New York, 1979), p. 169.

30 Paul Schullery, *American Bears: Selections from the Writings of Theodore Roosevelt* (Boulder, CO, 1983), pp. 20–23.

31 Quoted in *ibid.*, p. 59.

32 Quoted in *ibid.*, p. 62.

33 M. A. Ramsay, 'Cycles of Feasting and Fasting', in Ian Stirling, ed., *Bears*, p. 67.

34 Charles T. Feazel, *White Bear: Encounters with the Master of the Arctic Ice* (New York, 1990), pp. 30–31.

35 M. A. Ramsay, 'Winter Sleep', in Ian Stirling, ed., *Bears*, pp. 68–9.

36 Lynn Rogers, 'Home, Sweet-Smelling Home', *Natural History*

(September 1989), p. 62.

37 *Ibid.*, p. 66.

5 THE PACKAGED BEAR

1 Fred Bruemmer, 'Arctic Treasures', *Natural History* (June 1989), p. 41.

2 Keith Thomas, *Man and the Natural World: A History of the Modern Sensibility* (New York, 1983), pp. 144–58.

3 Quoted in *ibid*.

4 Paul Shepard and Barry Sanders, *The Sacred Paw: The Bear in Nature, Myth, and Literature* (New York, 1985), pp. 56–7.

5 Alison Ames, 'Dancing Bears', in Ian Stirling, ed., *Bears* (San Francisco, 1993), pp. 204–5.

6 Olaus Magnus, *Description of the Northern Peoples*, ed. Peter Foote, trans. Peter Fisher and Humphrey Higgins (London, 1998),

7 'Activists Free Dancing Bears', *International Herald Tribune* (8 June 2004), p. A7.

8 Hannes Sägesser, *La fosse aux ours de Berne* (Bern, 1982), pp. 1–3.

9 Andrew E. Derocher, 'Grizzly Adams', in Ian Stirling, ed., *Bears*, p. 220.

10 Jeff Fair, *The Great American Bear* (Minocqua, WI, 1990), pp. 167–9.

11 Erwin A. Bauer, *Bears: Behavior, Ecology, Conservation* (Stillwater, MN, 1996), p. 49.

12 Carroll Smith-Rosenberg, *Disorderly Conduct: Visions of Gender in Victorian America* (New York, 1985), p. 96.

13 David Quammen, *Monster of God* (New York, 2003), pp. 236–54.

14 Quoted in John G. Samson, ed., *The Worlds of Ernest Thompson Seton* (New York, 1976), p. 55.

15 Shepard and Sanders, *The Sacred Paw*, p. 154.

16 Edmund Morris, *Theodore Rex* (New York, 2002), pp. 172–3.

17 Philippa Waring, *In Praise of Teddy Bears* (London, 1980), pp. 31–44.

18 Sue Grant, '100 Years – Steiff Teddy Bears', *German Life* (December 2002/January 2003), pp. 38–9.

19 *Ibid*.

20 *Ibid*., pp. 107–9.

21 Quoted in Marty Crisp, *Teddy Bears in Advertizing Art* (Cumberland, MD, 1991), p. 63.

22 *Ibid*., p. 4.

23 *Ibid*.

24 *Ibid*., pp. 5, 8.

6 ROAD TO EXTINCTION?

1 Martha Hodgkin Green, 'Continental Divides', *Nature Conservancy* (January/February 2002), pp. 18–25.

2 John W. Schoen, Sterling D. Miller and Harry V. Reynolds, 'Last Stronghold of the Grizzly', *Natural History* (January 1987), pp. 54–5.

3 *Ibid*., p. 60.

4 Tom Walker, 'On Thin Ice', *Defenders* (Fall 2001), pp. 32–5.

5 Theo Colborn, Dianne Dumanoski and John Peterson Myers, *Our Stolen Future* (New York, 1996), pp. 87–9.

6 *Ibid*., p. 34.

7 Marla Cone, 'Bear Trouble', *Smithsonian Magazine* (April 2003), p. 73.

8 Yvonne Baskin, 'Trouble at Timberline', *Natural History* (November 1998), pp. 50–55.

9 Kerry Gunther, *Grizzly Bear Briefing Statement, Yellowstone National Park* (Yellowstone National Park, 2001), p. 3.

10 *Ibid*.

11 Gary Turbak, 'Food for Thought: What Does the Future Hold for Yellowstone's Grizzlies?', *National Wildlife*, vol. XXXVIII (October/November 2000), pp. 42–6.

12 Judy A. Mills and Christopher Servheen, *The Asian Trade in Bears and Bear Parts* (Washington, DC, 1991), pp. 80–81.

13 *Ibid*., p. 18.

14 *Ibid*., pp. 28–9.

15 *Ibid*., p. 30.

16 *Ibid.*, p. 81.

17 *Ibid.*, pp. 57–8.

18 *Ibid.*, p. 57.

19 Sy Montgomery, *Search for the Golden Bear: Science and Adventure in Pursuit of a New Species* (New York, 2002), pp. 32–3.

20 Mills and Servheen, *The Asian Trade in Bears*, p. 70.

21 Edward Topsell, *The History of Four-Footed Beasts and Serpents and Insects* (New York, 1967), p. 31.

22 Judy A. Mills, 'Bears as Pets, Food and Medicine', in Ian Stirling, ed., *Bears* (San Francisco, 1993), p. 122.

23 Montgomery, *Search for the Golden Bear*, p. 33.

24 Mills and Servheen, *The Asian Trade in Bears*, p. 70.

25 *Ibid.*

26 *Ibid.*, p. 60.

27 *Ibid.*, p. 73.

28 Mark R. Stanley Price, 'Reconstructing Ecosystems', in David Western and Mary Pearl, eds, *Conservation for the Twenty-first Century* (New York, 1989), pp. 210–18.

29 Terry Domico, *Bears of the World* (New York, 1988), pp. 107–8.

30 Diana Weinhardt, 'The Spectacled Bear', in Stirling, *Bears*, pp. 136–9

31 *Ibid.*, p. 139.

32 Stephen Fry, *Rescuing the Spectacled Bear* (London, 2002), pp. 76–80.

33 Christopher Servheen, 'The Future of Bears in the Wild', in Stirling, *Bears*, pp. 220–21.

34 Ian Stirling, 'The International Agreement on the Conservation of Polar Bears', in Stirling, *Bears*, pp. 230–31.

35 *Ibid.*, p. 231.

36 Fry, *Rescuing the Spectacled Bear*, p. 18.

37 Servheen, 'The Future of Bears', in Stirling, *Bears*, p. 212.

Bibliography

'Activists Free Dancing Bears,' *International Herald Tribune* (8 June 2004)

Barber, Richard, ed. and trans., *Bestiary: Being an English Version of the Bodleian Library, Oxford M.S. Bodley 764* (Woodbridge, Suffolk, 1992)

Baskin, Yvonne, 'Trouble at Timberline', *Natural History* (November 1998)

Bauer, Erwin, *Bears: Behavior, Ecology, Conservation* (Shrewsbury, 1996)

Becklund, Jack, *Summers with the Bears: Six Seasons in the North Woods* (New York, 1999)

Brodrick, A. Houghton, ed., *Animals in Archaeology* (New York, 1972)

Bruemmer, Fred, 'Arctic Treasures', *Natural History* (June 1989)

Clark, Ella E., *Indian Legends of the Pacific Northwest* (Berkeley, CA, 1965)

Colborn, Theo, Dianne Dumanoski and John Peterson Myers, *Our Stolen Future* (New York, 1996)

Cone, Marla, 'Bear Trouble', *Smithsonian* (April 2003)

Craighead, John J., Jay Sumner and John A. Mitchell, *Grizzly Bears of Yellowstone: Their Ecology in the Yellowstone Ecosystem, 1959–1992* (Washington, DC, 1995)

Crisp, Marty, *Teddy Bears in Advertising Art* (Cumberland, MD, 1991)

Domico, Terry, *Bears of the World* (New York, 1988)

Edsman, Carl-Martin, 'The Story of the Bear Wife in Nordic Tradition', *Ethnos*, XXI (1956)

Fair, Jeff, *The Great American Bear* (Minocqua, WI, 1990)

Feazel, Charles T., *White Bear: Encounters with the Master of the Arctic Ice* (New York, 1990)

Fry, Stephen, *Rescuing the Spectacled Bear* (London, 2002)

Gould, Stephen Jay, 'The Panda's Thumb', in Stephen Jay Gould, *The Panda's Thumb*, (New York, 1980)

Grant, Sue, '100 Years – Steiff Teddy Bears', *German Life* (December 2002/January 2003)

Green, Martha Hodgkins, 'Continental Divides', *Nature Conservancy* (January/February, 2002)

Gunther, Kerry, 'Bear Management in Yellowstone National Park, 1960–93', *International Conference on Bear Research and Management* (1994), vol. ix

Hallowell, A. Irving, 'Bear Ceremonialism in the Northern Hemisphere', *American Anthropologist*, n.s., xxviii (January–March 1926)

Harrison, Jane and Hope Mirrless, eds, *The Book of Bears* (London, 1926)

Haverstock, Mary Sayre, *An American Bestiary* (New York, 1979)

Honko, Lauri, Senni Timonen, Michael Branch, ed., *The Great Bear: A Thematic Anthology of Oral Poetry in Finno-Ugrian Languages*, trans. Keith Bosley (Helsinki, 1993)

Jardine, Sir William, ed., *The Naturalist's Library*, vol. xv (Edinburgh, 1840)

Kilham, Benjamin, *Among the Bears: Raising Orphan Cubs in the Wild* (New York, 2002)

Kurtén, Björn, *The Cave Bear Story: Life and Death of a Vanished Animal* (New York, 1976)

Lauwerier, Roel C.G.M. and Ina Plug, eds, *The Future From the Past* (Oxford, 2002)

Lönnrot, Elias ed., *The Kalevala*, trans. Keith Bosley (Oxford, 1989)

Lopez, Barry, *Arctic Dreams: Imagination and Desire in a Northern Landscape* (New York, 1986)

Loucks, Georgina, 'The Girl and the Bear Facts: A Cross-Cultural Comparison', *The Canadian Journal of Native Studies*, v (1985)

Magnus, Albertus, *On Animals: A Medieval 'Summa Zoologica'*, trans.

Kenneth F. Kitchell, Jr and Irven Michael Resnick (Baltimore, 1991)

Magnus, Olaus, *Description of the Northern Peoples*, ed. Peter Foote, trans. Peter Fisher and Humphrey Higgins (London, 1998)

Marriott, Alice and Carol K. Rachin, eds, *American Indian Mythology* (New York, 1968)

Mills, Judy A. and Christopher Servheen, *The Asian Trade in Bears and Bear Parts* (Washington, DC, 1991)

Milovsky, Alexander, 'Hail to Thee, Papa Bear', *Natural History* (December 1993)

Montgomery, Sy, *Search for the Golden Moon Bear: Science and Adventure in Pursuit of a New Species* (New York, 2002)

Morris, Edmund, *Theodore Rex* (New York, 2002)

Morris, Ramona and Desmond Morris, *Men and Pandas* (New York, 1966)

Paulaharju, Samuli, *Sommpio* (Helsinki, 1939)

Quammen, David, *Monster of God* (New York, 2003)

Ringer, Árpád, 'Kultuszok és müvészet', in Gyula Gyenis, Attila Hevesi, László Kordos, Árpád Ringer and Viola T. Dobosi, eds, *Emberelödök Nyomaban* (Miskolc, 2001)

Rockwell, David, *Giving Voice to the Bear: North American Rituals, Myths, and Images of the Bear* (Niwat, CO, 1991)

Rogers, Lynn, 'Home, Sweet-Smelling Home', *Natural History* (September 1989)

Roderick, A. Houghton, ed., *Animals in Archaeology* (New York, 1972)

Sägesser, Hannes, *La fosse aux ours de Berne* (Bern, 1982)

Salisbury, Joyce E., *The Beast Within: Animals in the Middle Ages* (New York, 1994)

—— ed., *The Medieval World of Animals: A Book of Essays* (New York, 1993)

Samson, John G., ed., The *World of Ernest Thompson Seton* (New York, 1976)

Schaller, George B., *The Last Panda* (Chicago, 1994)

Schoen, John W., Stirling D. Miller, and Harry V. Reynolds III, eds, 'Last Stronghold of the Grizzly', *Natural History* (January 1987)

Schullery, Paul, ed., *American Bears: Selections from the Writings of Theodore Roosevelt* (Boulder, CO, 1983)

Shepard, Paul and Barry Sanders, *The Sacred Paw: The Bear in Nature, Myth, and Literature* (New York, 1985)

Smith-Rosenberg, Carroll, *Disorderly Conduct: Visions of Gender in Victorian America* (New York, 1985)

Stirling, Ian, ed., *Bears* (San Francisco, 1993)

Thomas, Keith, *Man and the Natural World: A History of Modern Sensibility* (New York, 1983)

Thwaites, Reuben Gold, ed., *Original Journals of the Lewis and Clark Expedition, 1804–1806* (New York, 1959), vol. I

Topsell, Edward, *The History of Four-Footed Beasts and Serpents and Insects* (reprinted New York, 1967), vol. I

Toynbee, J.M.C., *Animals in Roman Life and Art* (Ithaca, NY, 1973)

Turbak, Gary, 'Food for Thought: What Does the Future Hold for Yellowstone's Grizzlies?', *National Wildlife*, XXXVIII (October/November 2000)

Walker, Tom, 'On Thin Ice', *Defenders* (Fall 2001)

Waring, Philippa, *In Praise of Teddy Bears* (London, 1997)

Western, David and Mary Pearl, eds, *Conservation for the Twenty-first Century* (New York, 1988)

Wolfe, Art, *Bears: Their Life and Behaviour* (1992)

Associations

BEAR PROTECTION NETWORK
PO Box 130130
Houston, Texas 77219-0130 USA

GREAT BEAR FOUNDATION
802 E. Front
Missoula, Montana 59802 USA

INTERNATIONAL ANIMAL RESCUE
Lime House
Regency Close
Uckfield, East Sussex TN22 1DS,
England, UK

NATIONAL WILDLIFE FEDERATION
11100 Wildlife Center Drive
Reston, Virginia, 20190-5362
USA

NATURE CONSERVANCY
4245 N. Fairfax Drive, Suite 100
Arlington, Virginia, 22203 USA

NORWEGIAN POLAR INSTITUTE
Polarmiljosenteret 9296
Tromso, Norway

THE WILDERNESS SOCIETY
1615 M Street NW
Washington, DC, 20036, USA

THE WORLD CONSERVATION
UNION (IUCN)
Rue Mouverney 28
CH 1196 Gland
Switzerland

Websites

www.bbc.co.uk/nature/wildfacts
> is the BBC's website on animals listed under Science and Nature. In addition to offering advice on mammals, sea life and birds, there are sections on pets and conservation

www.bears-bears.org
> provides facts on bear conservation, links to other sources and thousands of pictures of bears

www.bearden.org
> is run by the American Zoo and Aquarium Association. This site is part of AZAA's mission to promote conservation, education and research on various species of bear

www.bearbiology.com
> is the website of the International Association for Bear Research and Management, a non-profit volunteer organization dedicated to the conservation of all species of bear

Acknowledgements

I am a firm believer that books are written with the help of friends, jugs of coffee and gallons of tea. This book is no exception and I have enjoyed an abundance of all three. Foremost in the field of toil is Wendy Read Wertz, who put her life on hold in order to proof-read my text and put it into the computer. She also sat long hours going over the text with me and made my English comprehensible, offered encouragement and served up coffee and cookies. Without her labours and her enthusiasm for this project, it would still only be a good idea.

Help also came from my dear friend Zoltan Abádi-Nagy, who introduced me to László Kordos. It was László who guided me through the intricacies of how to interpret cave bear skulls and facilitated a trip to the Bükk Mountains where cave bear remains had been found. I thank them both.

Others suggested books, articles and artefacts that proved valuable to the construction of my tale. They include Riku Hamalainen, Susanne Österlund-Pötzsch, Mia Rehn, David Fahgy, Merike Holmberg, Gerhard Baer, Claudette 'Teddy' Latchford, Ann B. Hood and Judith Kenneweg Sturm.

Still others helped in translating from Finnish to English. Here especially I had the help of Rani Andersson. He also, despite illness, hiked through the Finnish forest with me and sat out a night in a cold blind, observing bears. My friend, Henrik Gustafsson, offered aid not only in translations from Swedish but also in the finer points of Swedish linguistics.

Help also came in other ways. Scholars, like armies, also travel on their stomachs. Friends in Hungary, Germany and Finland all spoiled me with their support and I greatly appreciate their generosity and goodwill. They include Imre, Csibi and Eva Becsei, Karen Goihl, Mia and Leila Rehn.

Also deserving of mention for their aid are: Indiana University Libraries, the British Museum, the National Museum of Finland, the Geological Museum of Hungary, the Lincoln Park Zoo of Chicago, and the Indianapolis Zoo. Their kindnesses in fulfilling my many requests for information are appreciated.

Finally, I would like to thank my editor, Jonathan Burt, and all those who listened to me talk ceaselessly about bears for two years and did not let it spoil our friendships. These include not only many of my students and most of those listed above but also, in particular, Maryellen Bieder, Kristina Rusnik, Roy Goldblatt and Martin Zanger.

My debt to all of you is enormous. I love you all.

Photo Acknowledgements

The author and publishers wish to express their thanks to the below sources of illustrative material and/or permission to reproduce it. (Some sources uncredited in the captions for reasons of brevity are also given below.)

Photo Ancient Art and Architecture Collection, Ltd/R. Sheridan: p. 84; graphic by the author: p. 147; photos courtesy of the author: pp. 8, 28 (top), 32, 33, 38, 69 (top), 79, 89, 90 (top), 132, 134 (foot); The Brooklyn Museum of Art: p. 77 (photo BMA Central Photo Archive, 12.688); Burke Museum of Natural History and Culture, University of Washington, Seattle: p. 100 (photos courtesy of the Burke Museum, catalogue # 25.0/212); Eiteljorg Museum of American Indians and Western Art, Indianapolis: p. 58 (left, 1989.30.35, right 1989.30.33, photos courtesy of the Eiteljorg Museum); Finnish Historical Society, Helsinki: p. 52 (photo courtesy of the National Board of Antiquities, Helsinki/Markku Haverinen 2004); photos courtesy of the Geological Institute of Hungary: pp. 13, 16, 20, 23; courtesy of the artist (Helena Junttila): pp. 57, 59, 62; photos courtesy of Claudette Latchford: pp. 25, 127, 128 (foot), 139; photos Library of Congress, Washington, DC: pp. 68 (Prints and Photographs Division, LC-USZC4-10058), 94 (National Photo Company Collection, LC-USZ62-100982), 87 top (National Photo Company Collection, LC-USZ62-59691), 106 (National Photo Company Collection, LC-USZC4-2630), 134 top (National Photo Company Collection, LC-USZC4-4440), 160 (Prints and Photographs Division, Work Projects Administration Poster Collection, LC-USZC4-4164); photos courtesy of The Lilly Library, Indiana University, Bloomington, IN: pp. 72, 119, 120, 123 (top), 131; The Mathers Museum of World Cultures, Bloomington, IN: pp. 39 top, 39 foot (photo Joseph Dixon), 64, 66, 69 foot; collection of the New-York Historical Society: p. 90 (foot); photo New York Public Library: p. 104; photos Rex Features: pp. 6 (Sipa Press, 160828A), 24 (Chris Martin Bahr, 358199A), 28 foot (Tom Brakefield, 457614A), 36 (Doug Plummer, 385824A), 63 (John Hannah, 68184B), 99 (Hugh Harrop, 268950B), 107 (Jeff Chagrin, 271172H), 108 (Jeff Chagrin, top 271172A, foot 271172G), 109 (Jeff Chagrin, top 271172B, foot 271172E), 110 (Graham Trott, 187491A), 123 foot (RUS, 284327E); 128 top (Clive Dixon, 149657A), 148 (WSBA, top 319653AM, foot 319653N), 149 (WSBA, 319653U), 167 Nukari [LHT], 425255A); The National Anthropological Archives (Smithsonian Institution), Suitland, MD: p. 60; State Tretyakov Gallery, Moscow: p. 138; photo Judith Kenneweg Sturm: p. 126; United States Postal Service (Displayed with permission. All rights reserved): p. 124; photos Roger Viollet/Rex Features: pp. 50 (© Collection Roger-Viollet, 6611-14), 111 ((© Collection Roger-Viollet, top 9111-9, foot 9169-11), 114 (top © Lipnitzki/Roger-Viollet, 5033-18, foot Harlinque/Roger-Viollet, 454227AY); 116 (photo © Collection Roger-Viollet, 14438-8), 117 (photo © ND/Roger-Viollet, 1283-13), p.130 (photo © LAP/Roger-Viollet, 3325-14), p.142 (9111-9); photos © Zoological Society of London: pp. 37, 91, 92.

Index